Die Große Groove Schule 4
Latin Jazz - Salsa - Songo
Independence Trainer

Die große Groove-Schule 4

Training & Sightreading for Professional

Jazz Latin - Salsa - Songo

Von: Thomas Stan Hemken   www.drums-online.org

IMPRESSUM

Bibliografische Information der Deutschen Nationalbibliothek:
Die Deutsche Nationalbibliothek verzeichnet diese Publikation in der Deutschen Nationalbibliografie; detaillierte bibliografische Daten sind im Internet über http://dnb.dnb.de abrufbar.

© 2017 Thomas Stan Hemken

www.drums-online.org
Herstellung und Verlag: BoD – Books on Demand, Norderstedt

ISBN: 9783743119314

Index

Latin Jazz Independence	1
Latin Jazz & Clave	10
Salsa Independence Lesson 1	11
Salsa Independence Lesson 2	20
Salsa Independence Lesson 3	29
Salsa Independence Lesson 4	39
Salsa Independence Lesson 5	48
Salsa Independence Lesson 6	58
Salsa Grooves & Claves	67

Latin Jazz Independence

Thomas Stan Hemken

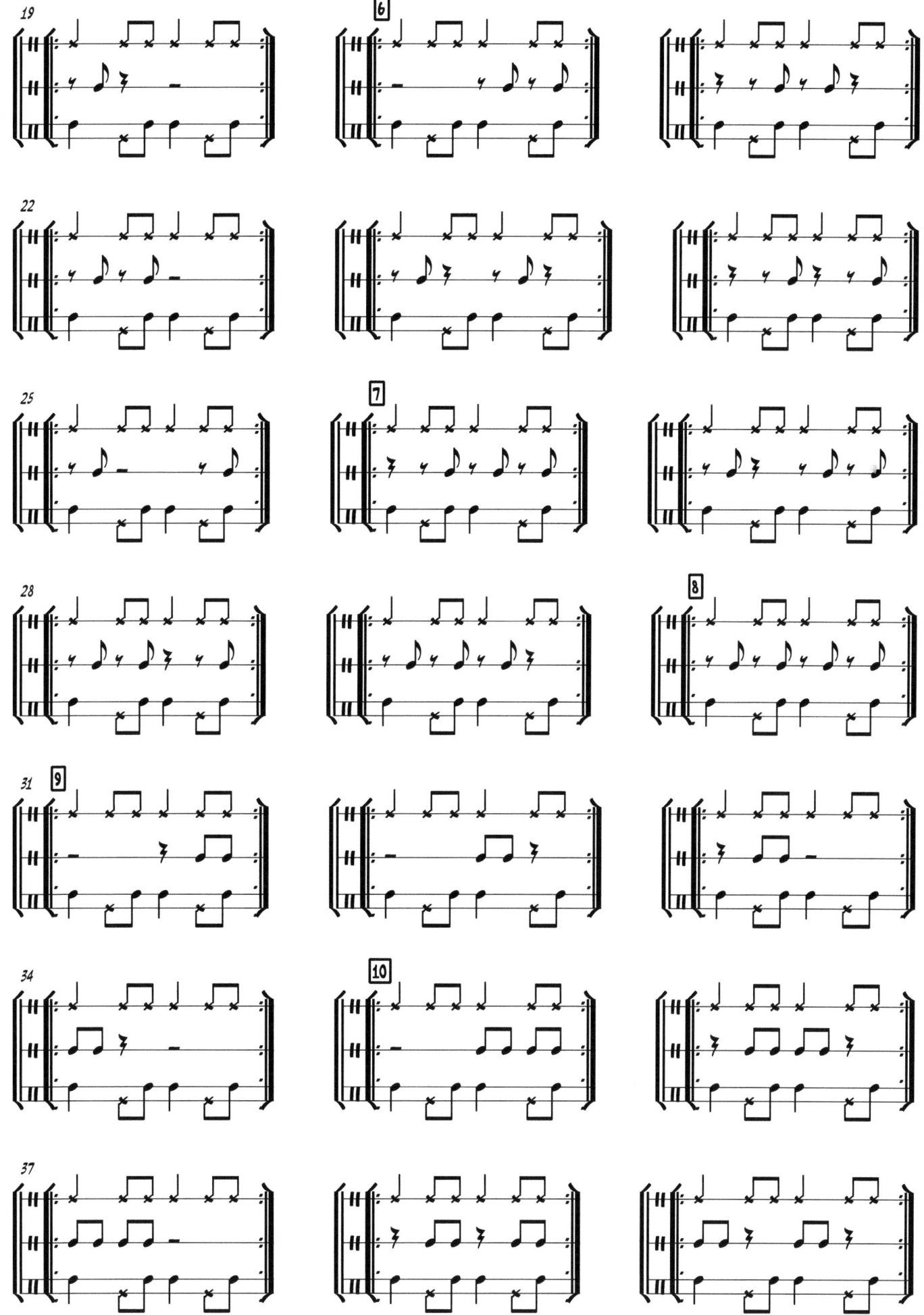

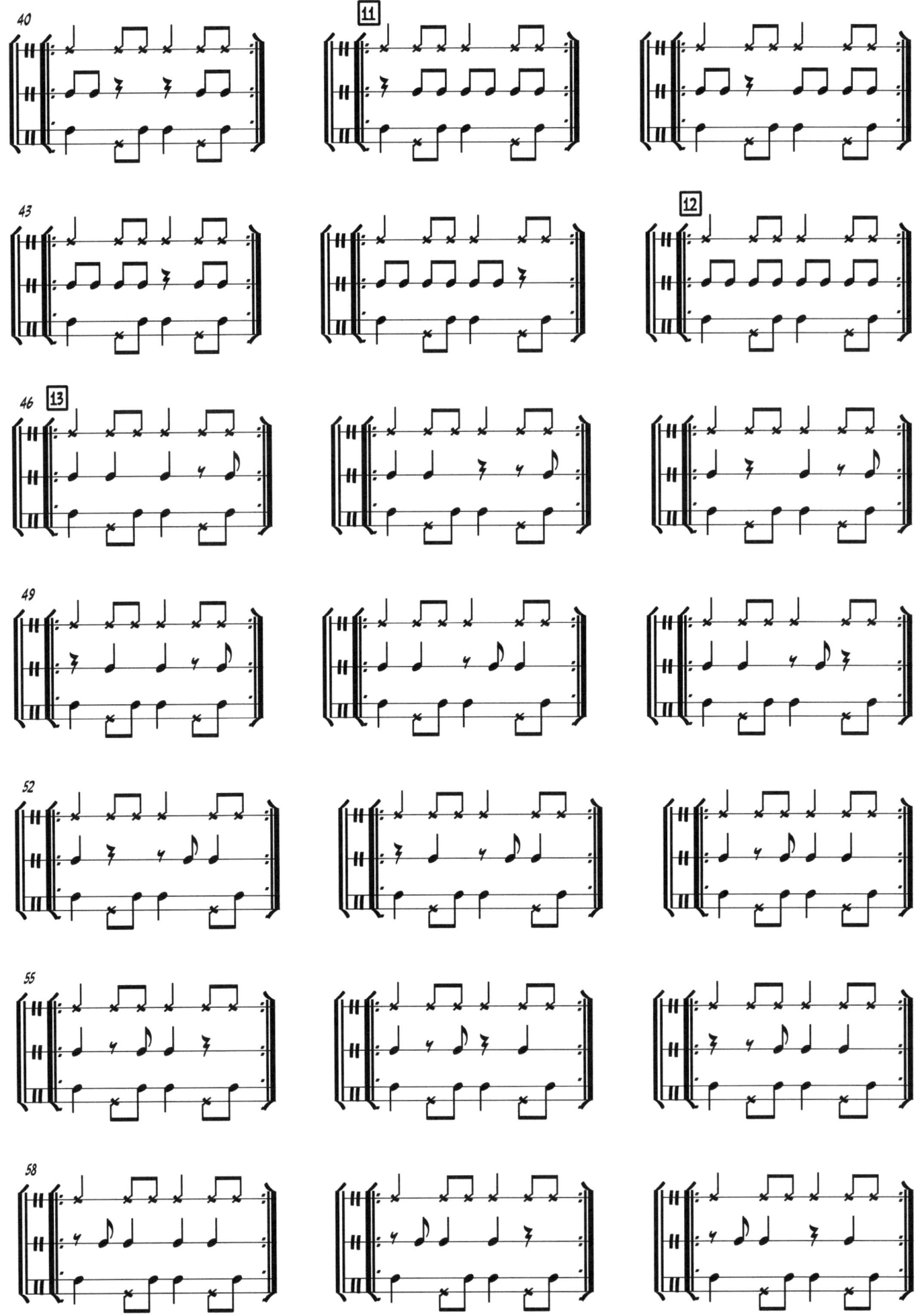

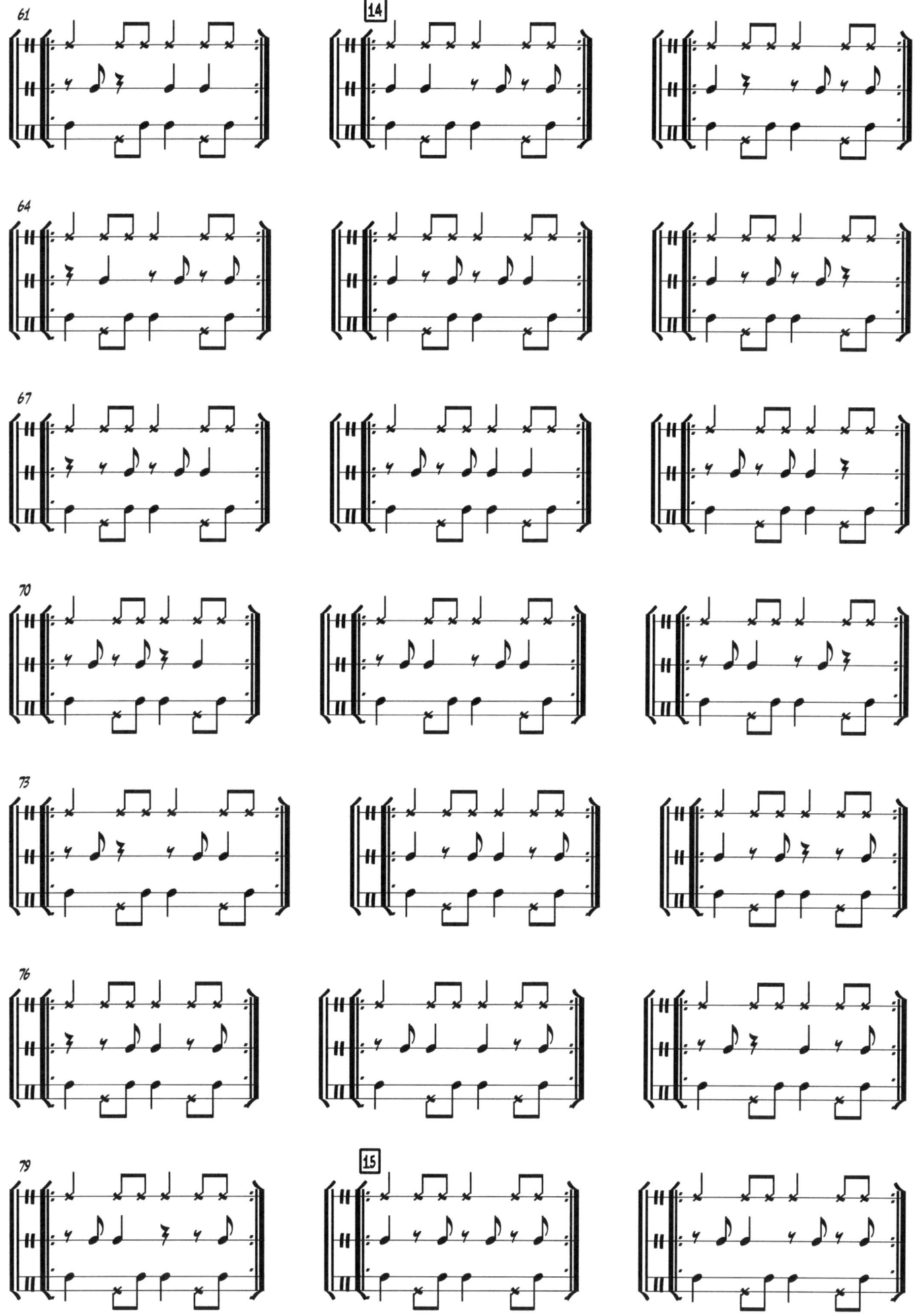

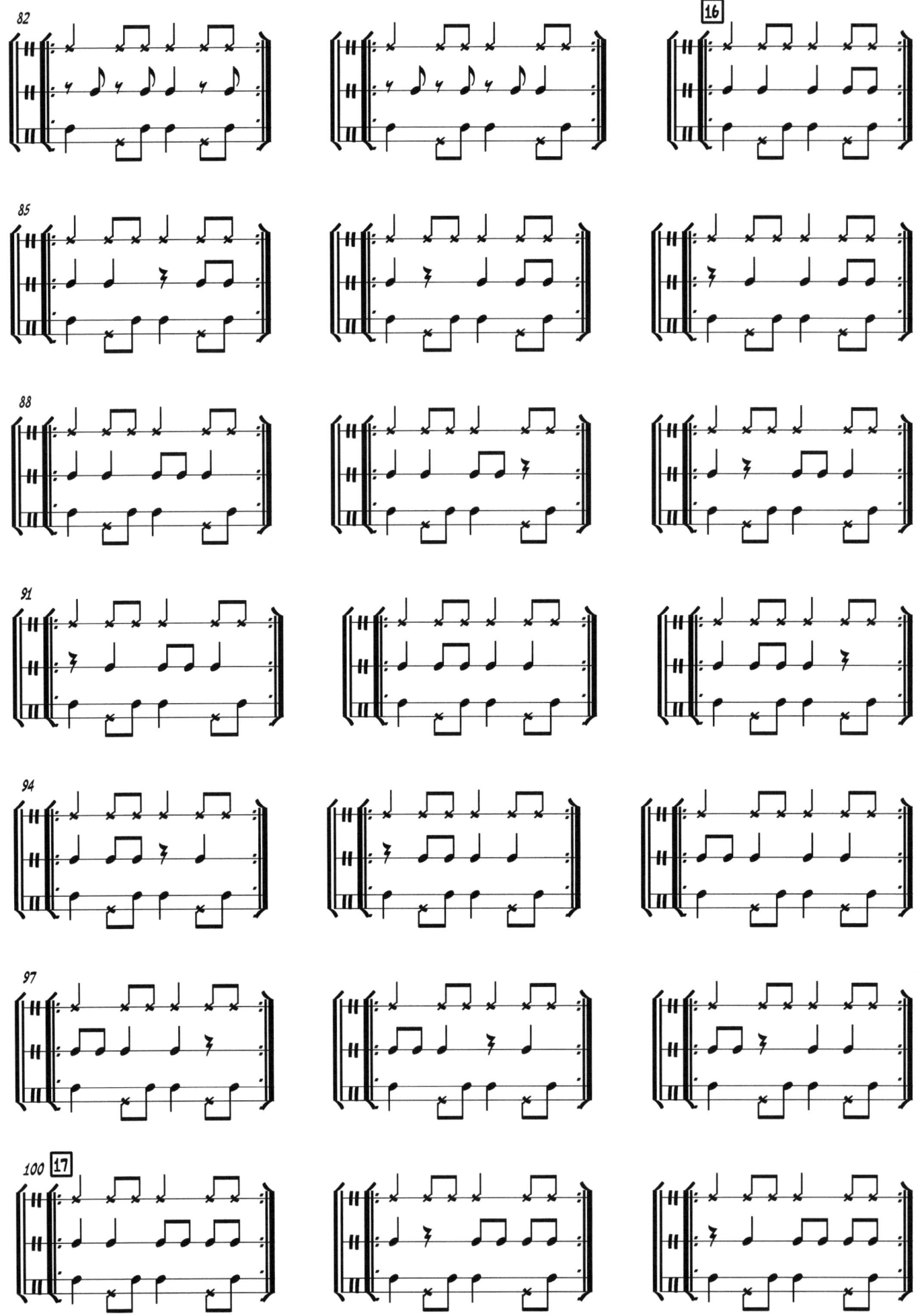

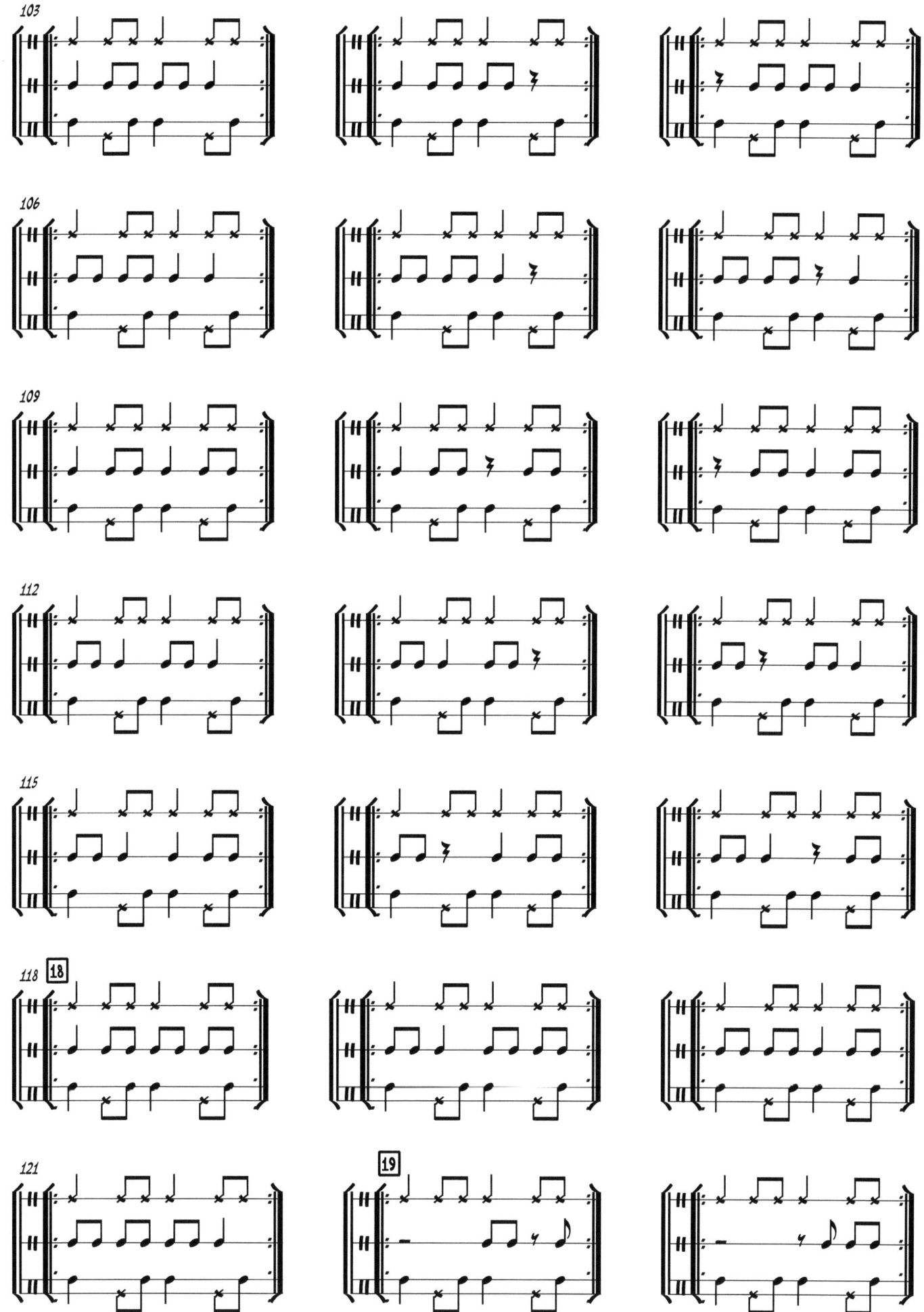

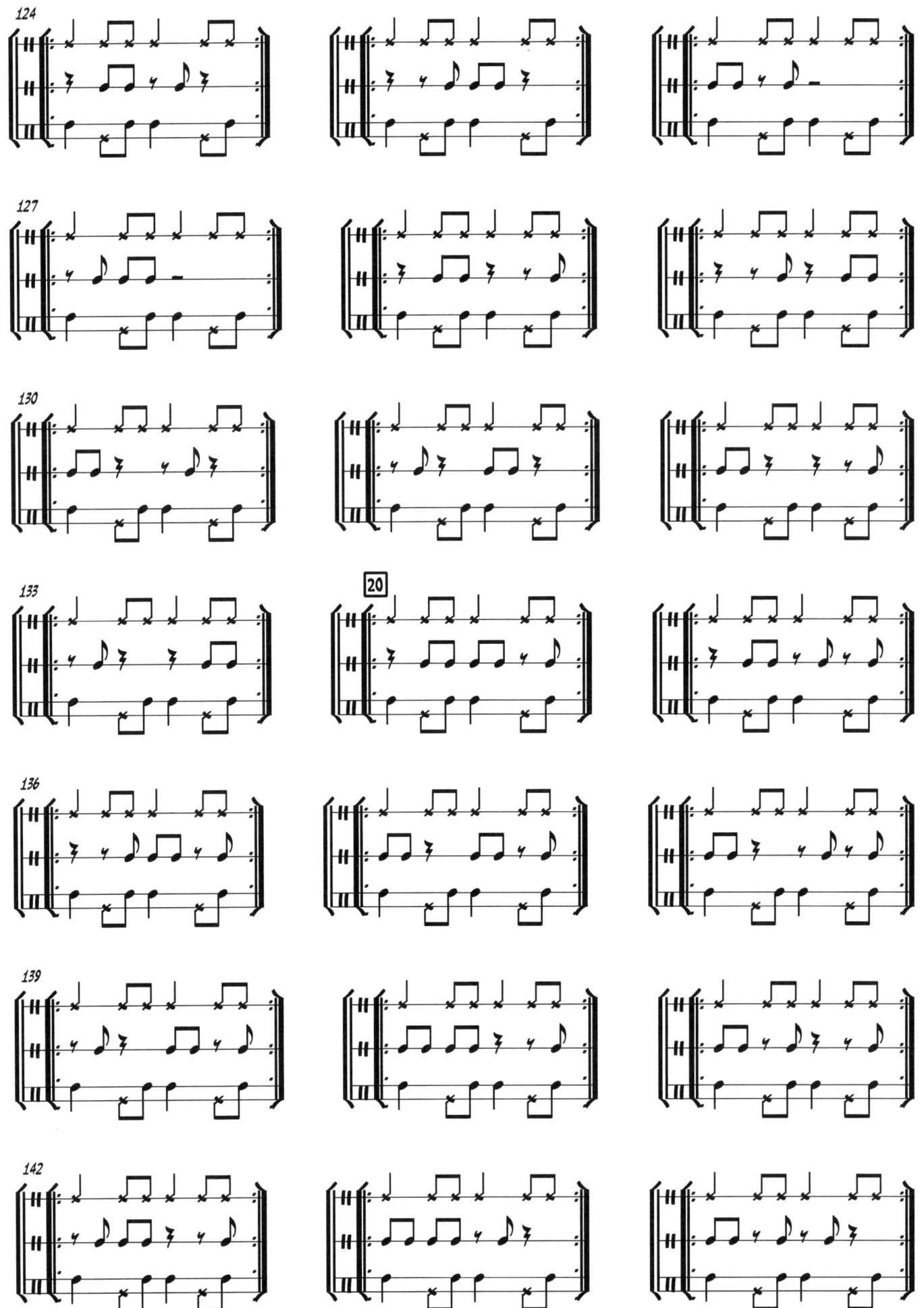

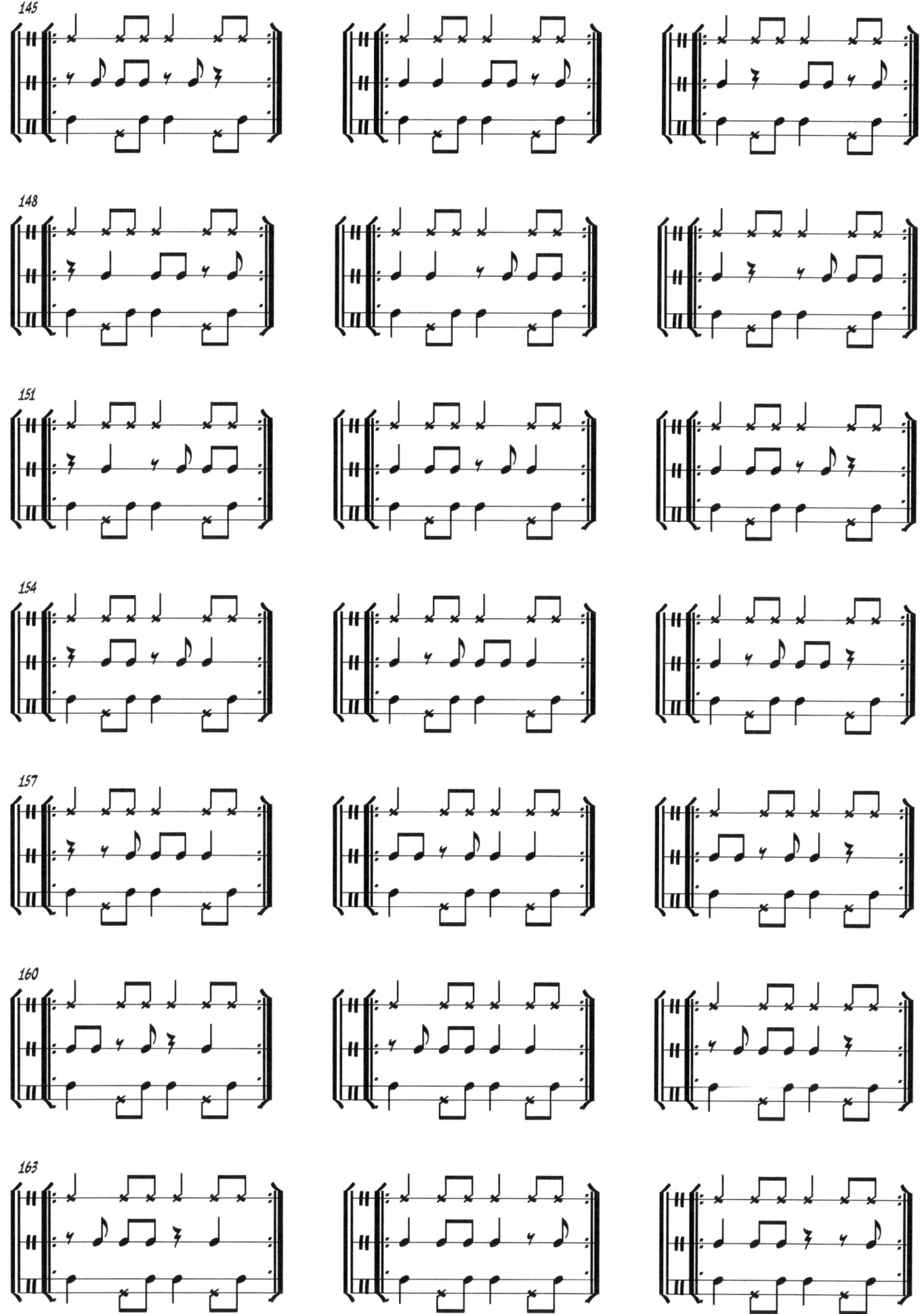

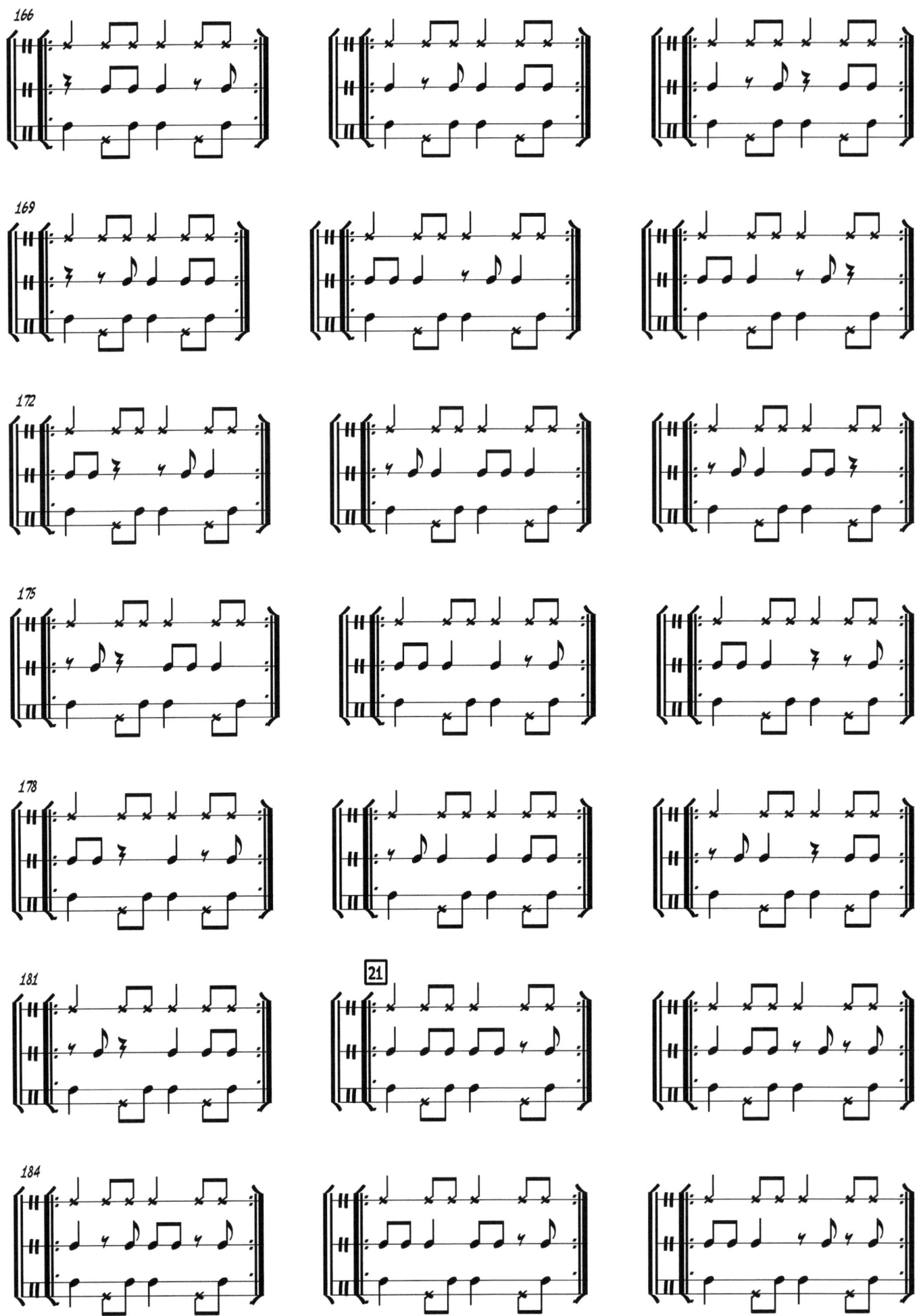

Salsa Indipendence

Drumset — Thomas Stan Hemken

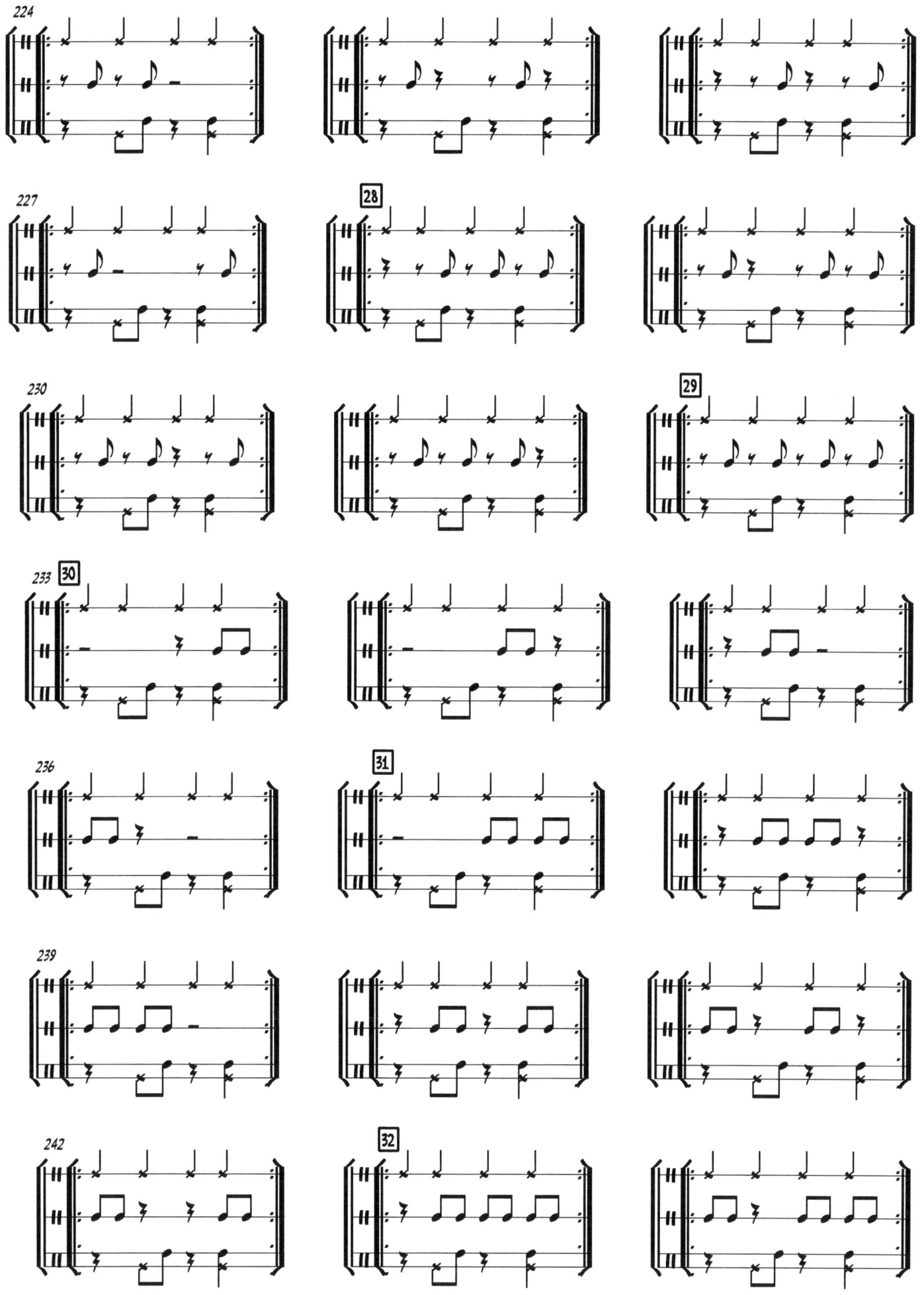

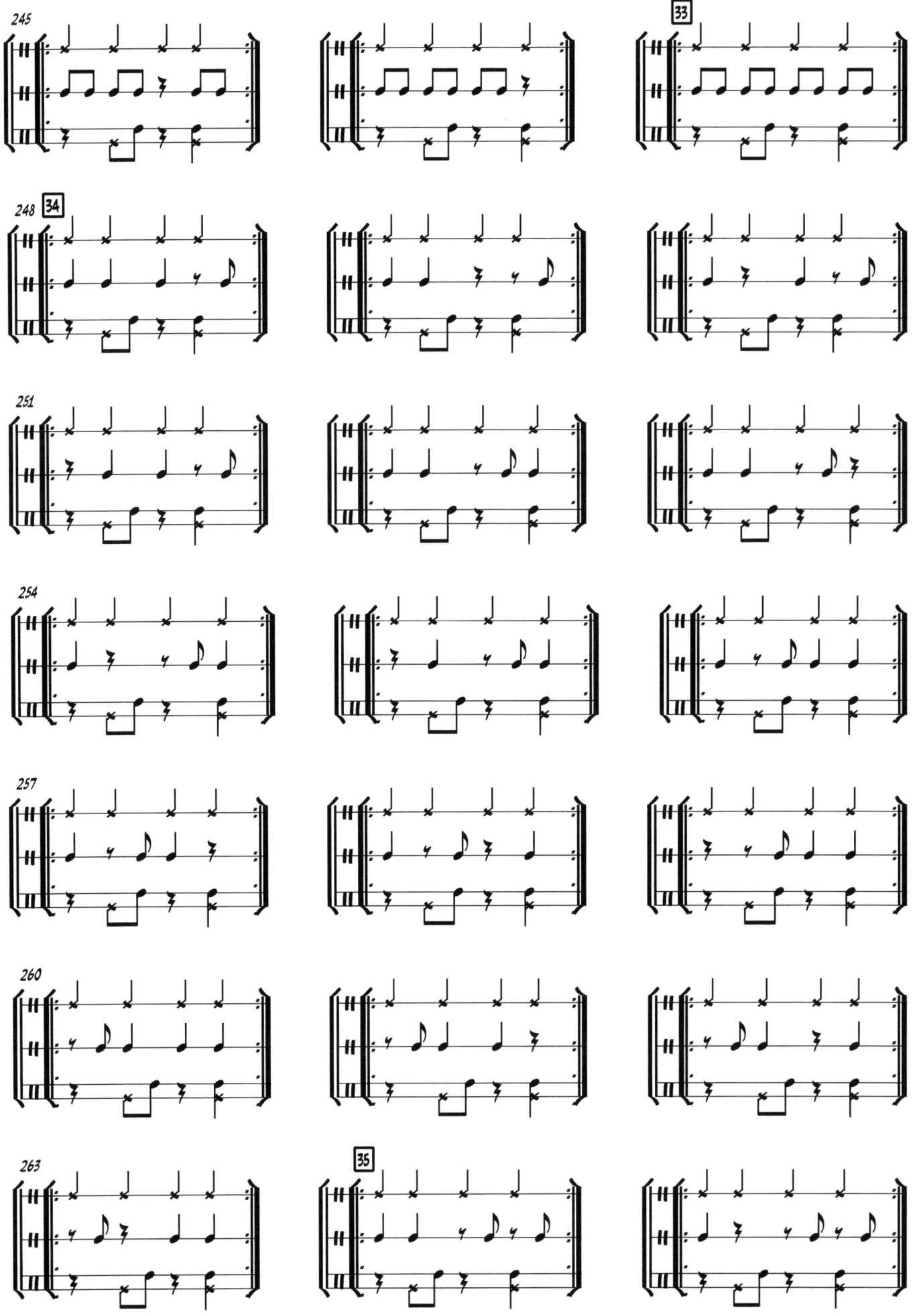

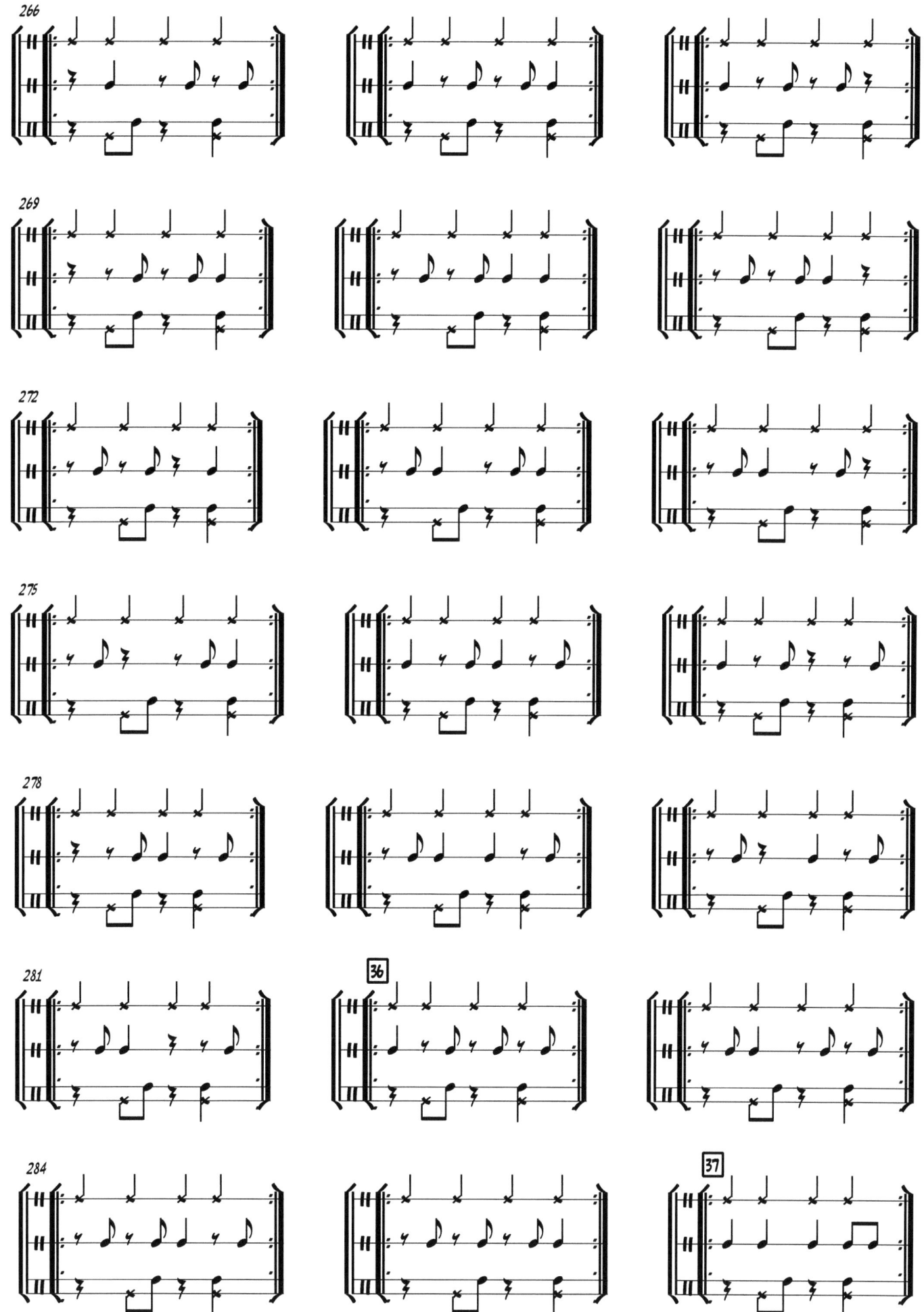

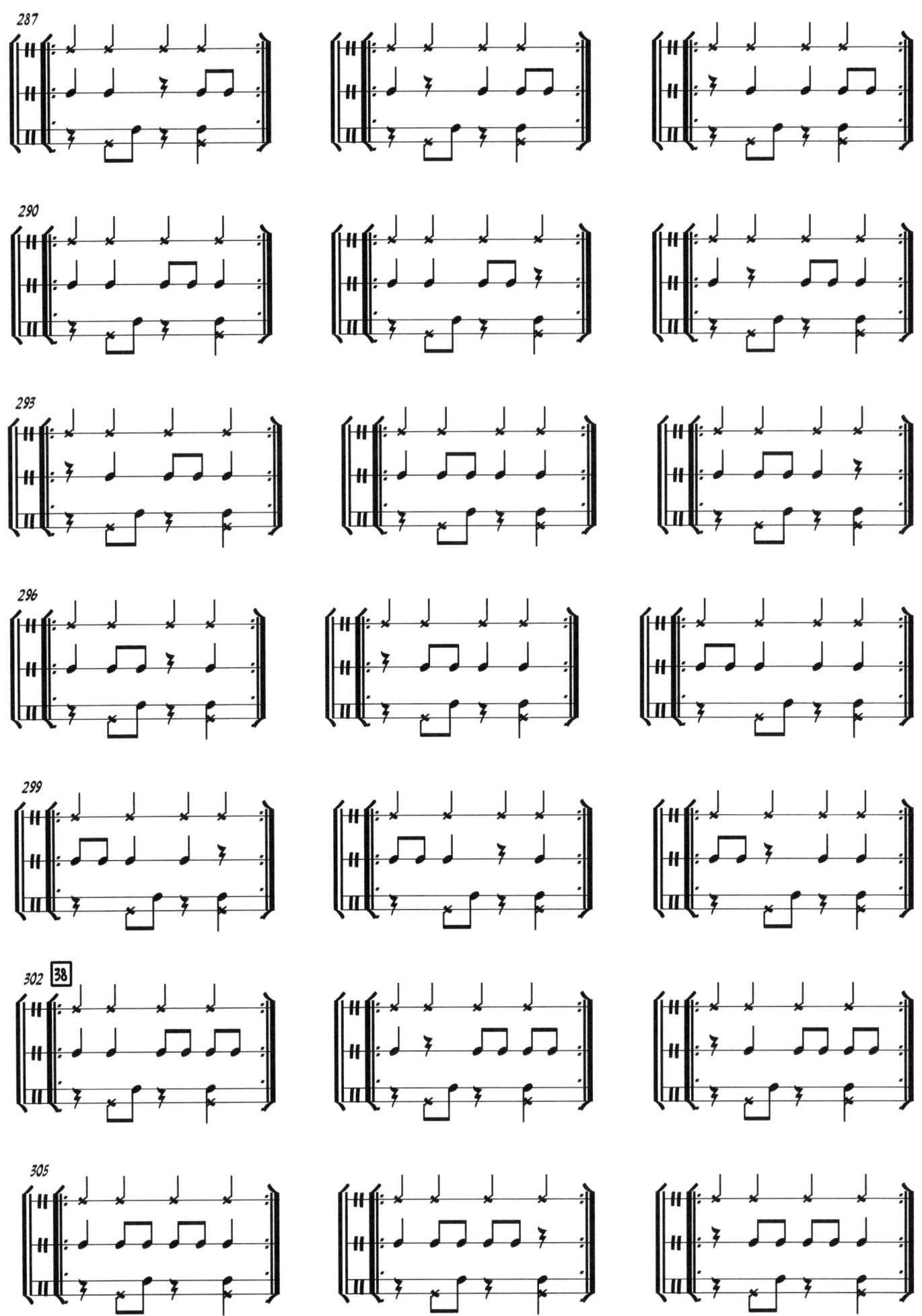

16

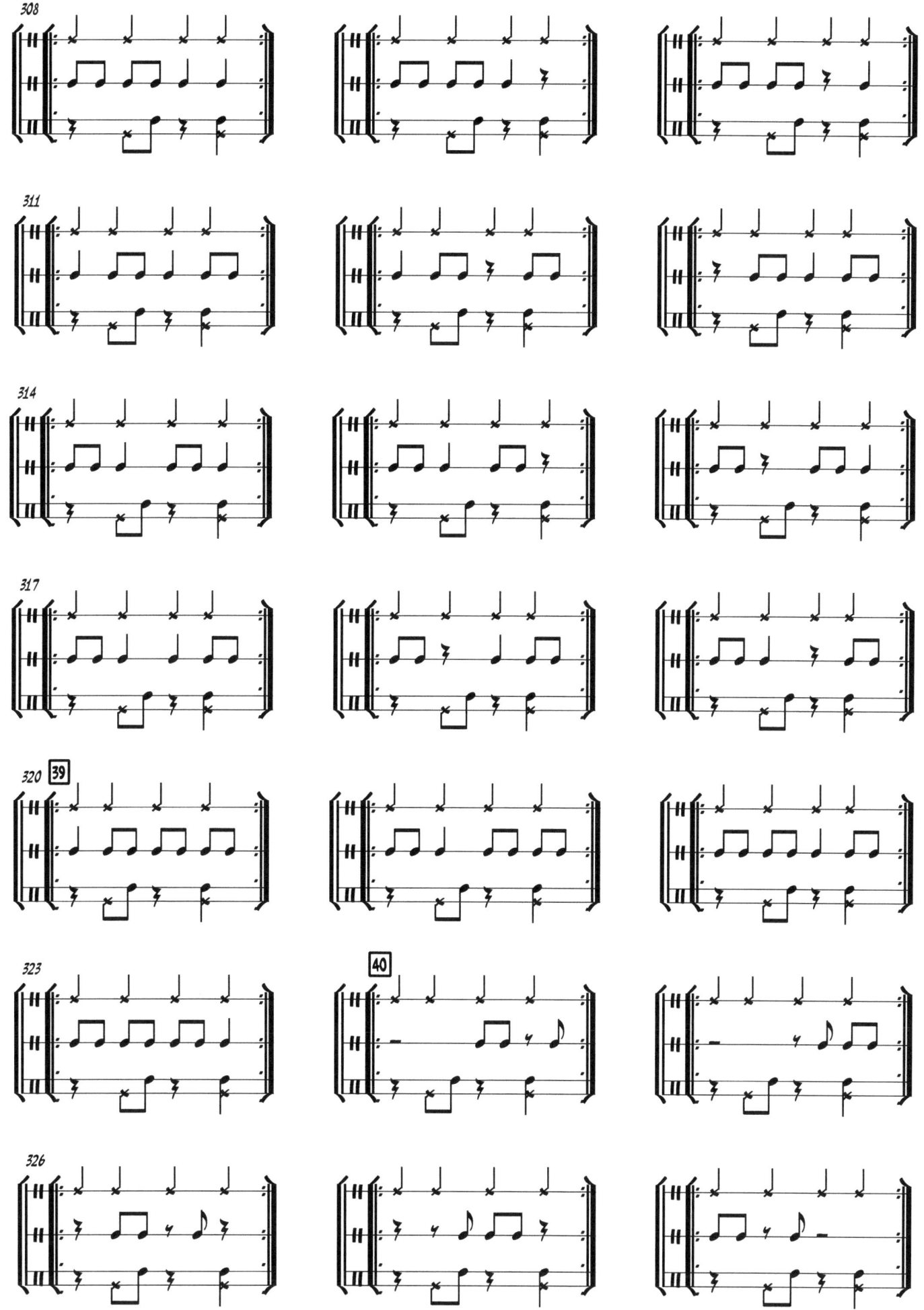

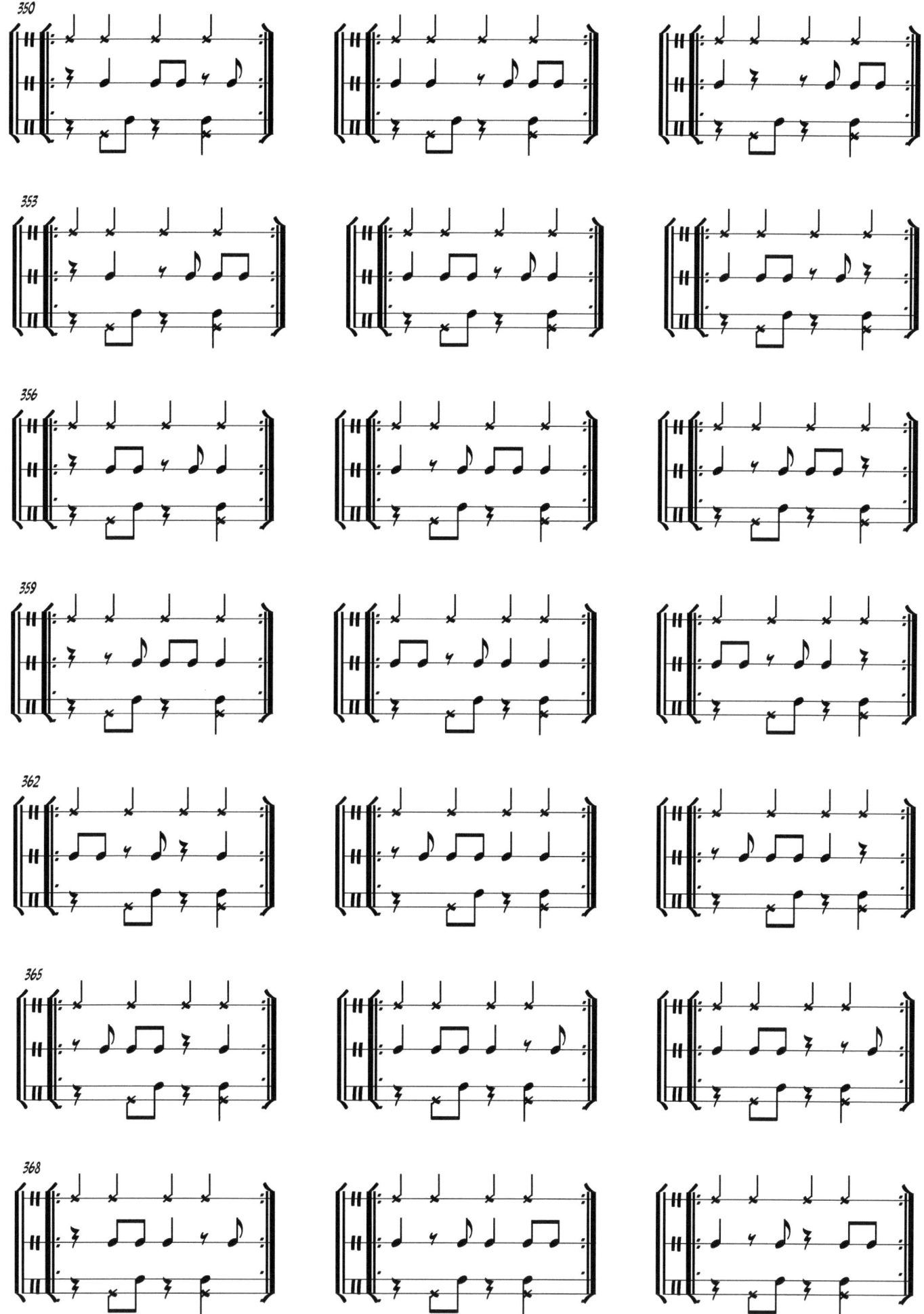

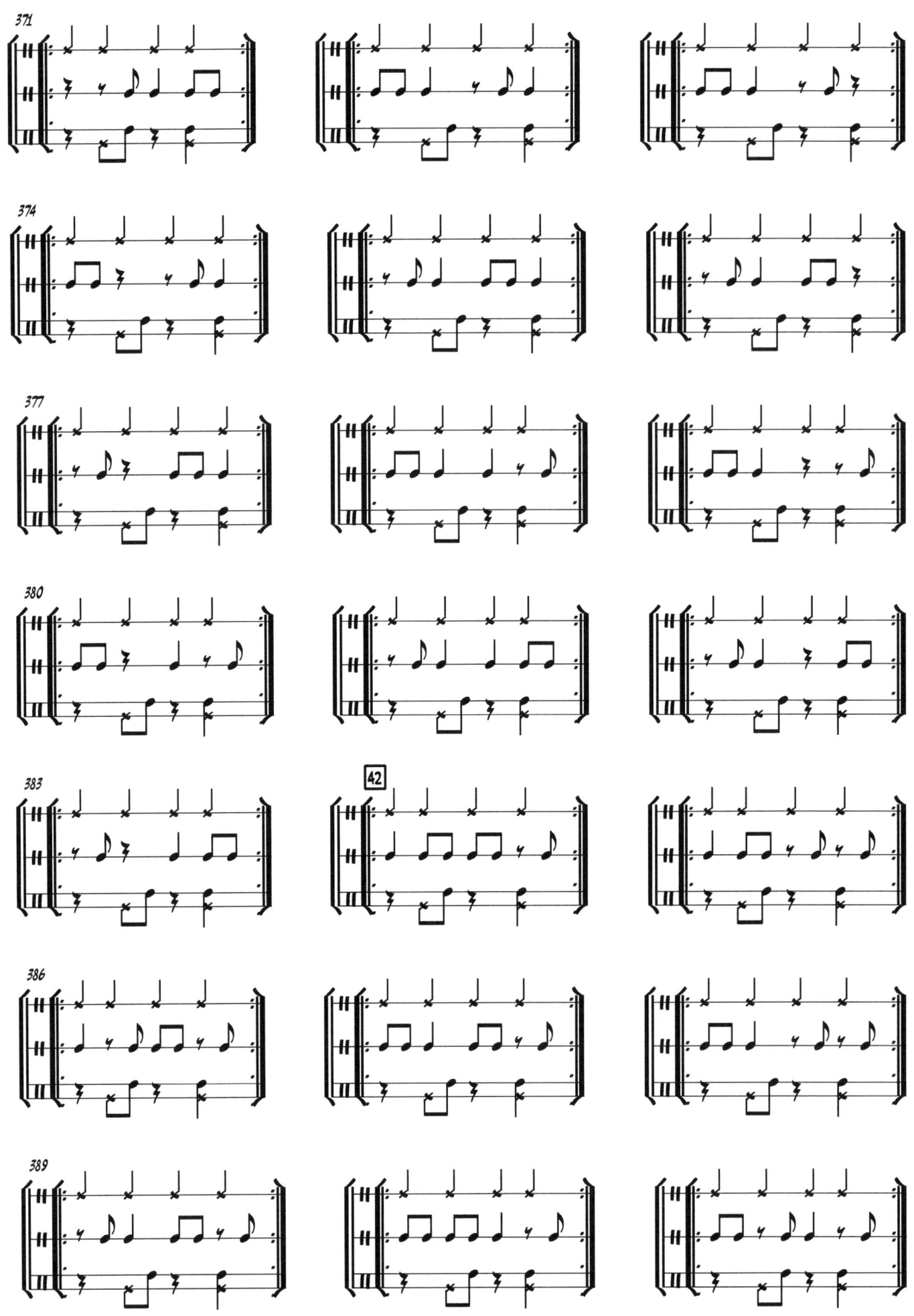

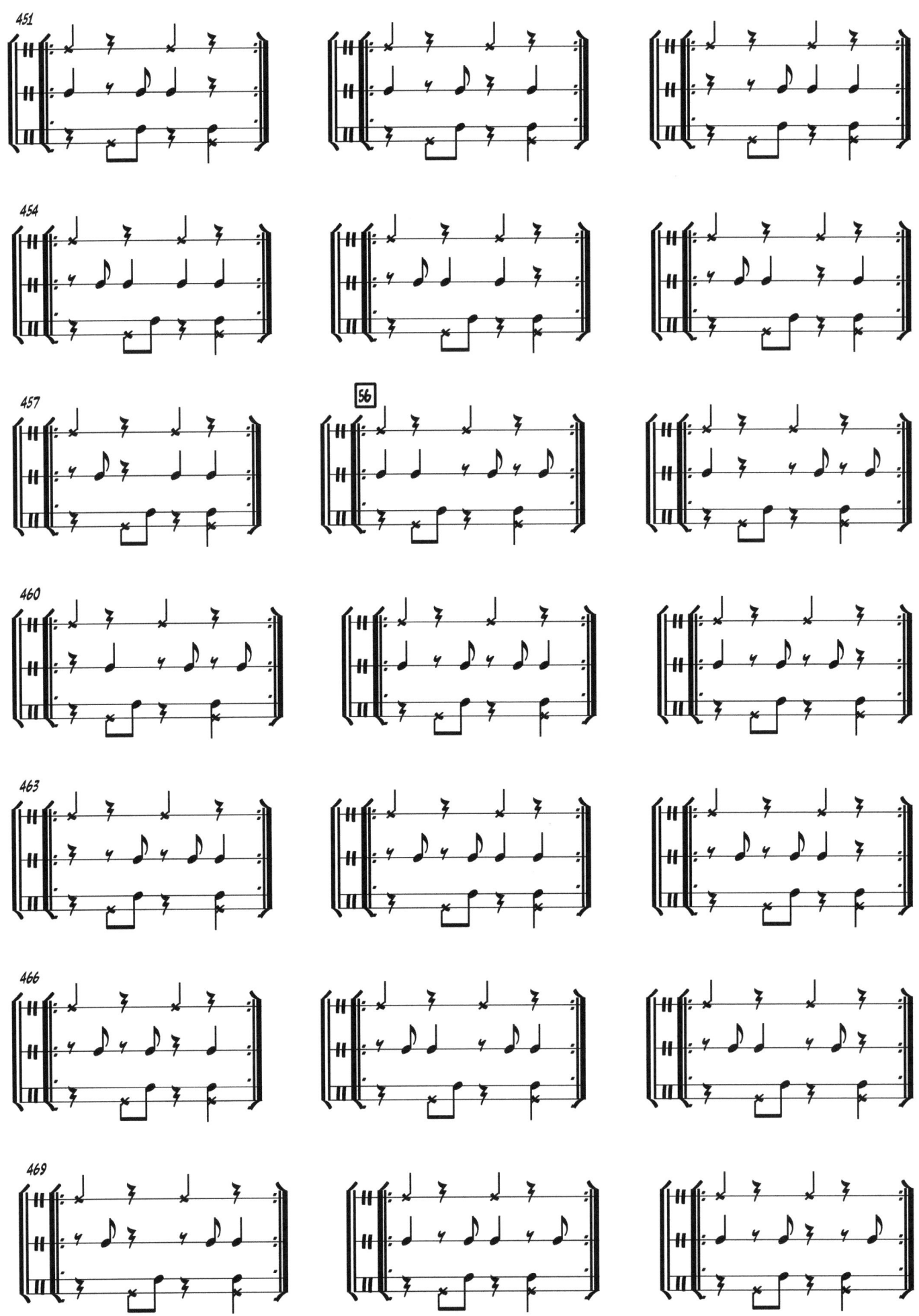

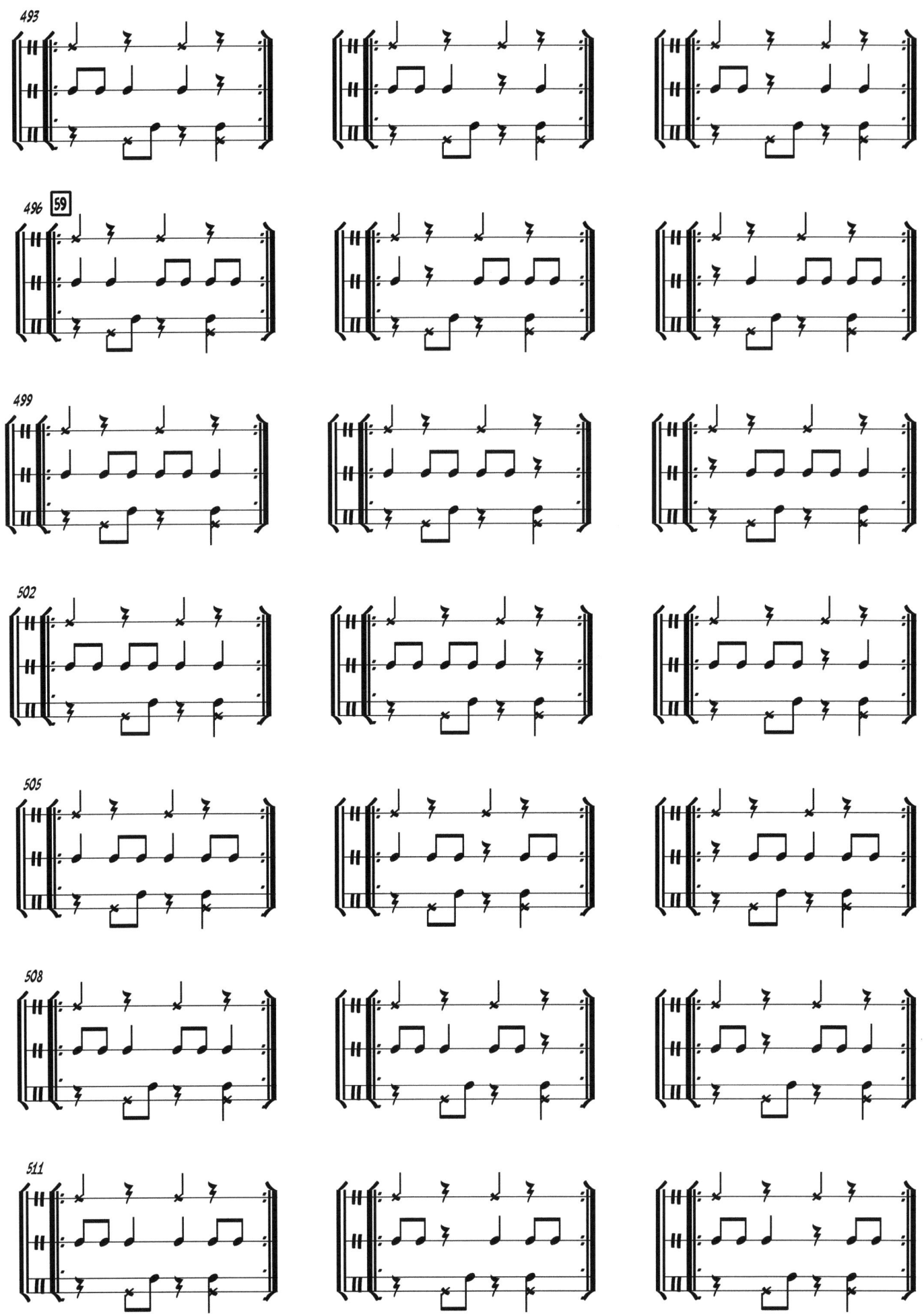

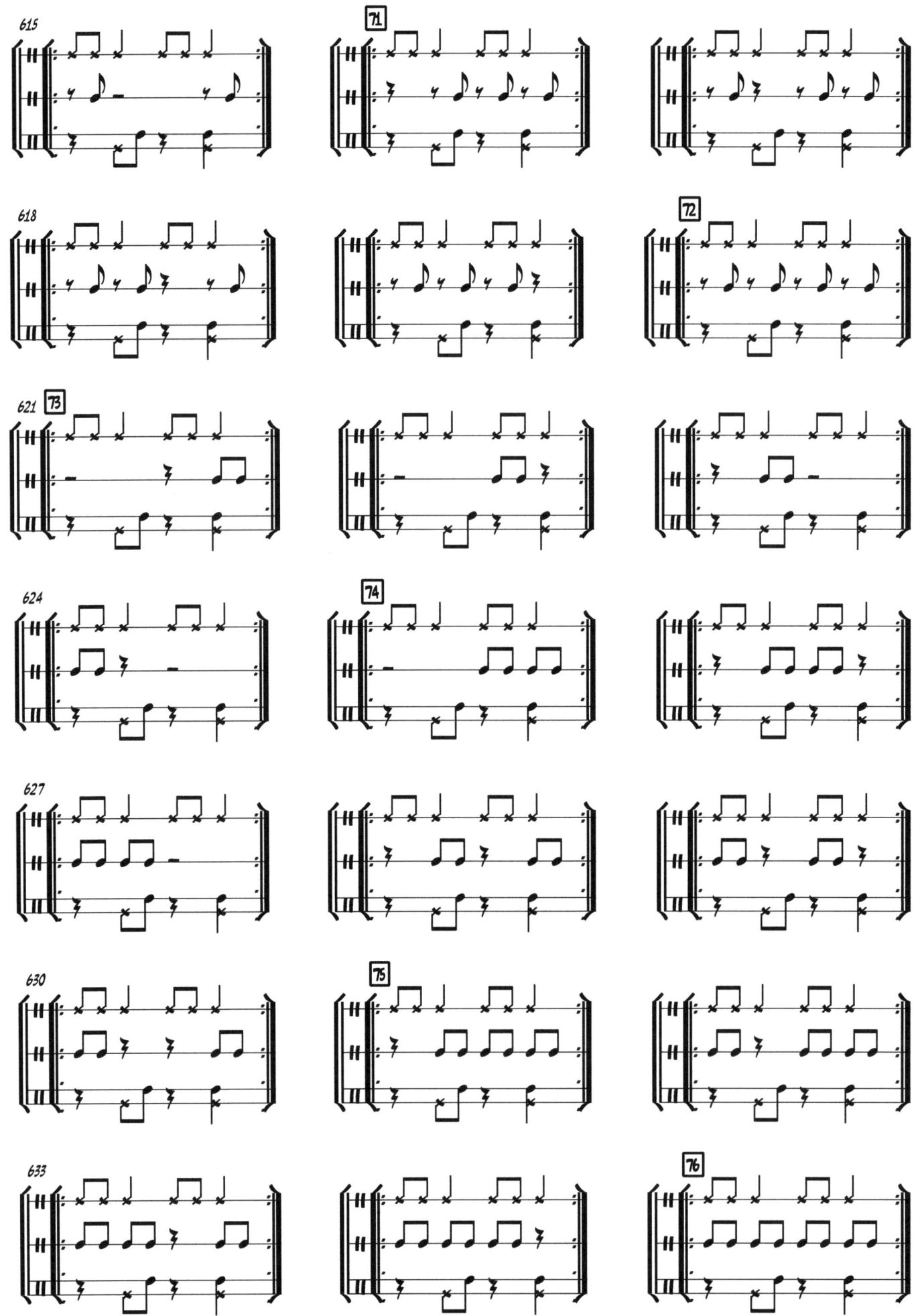

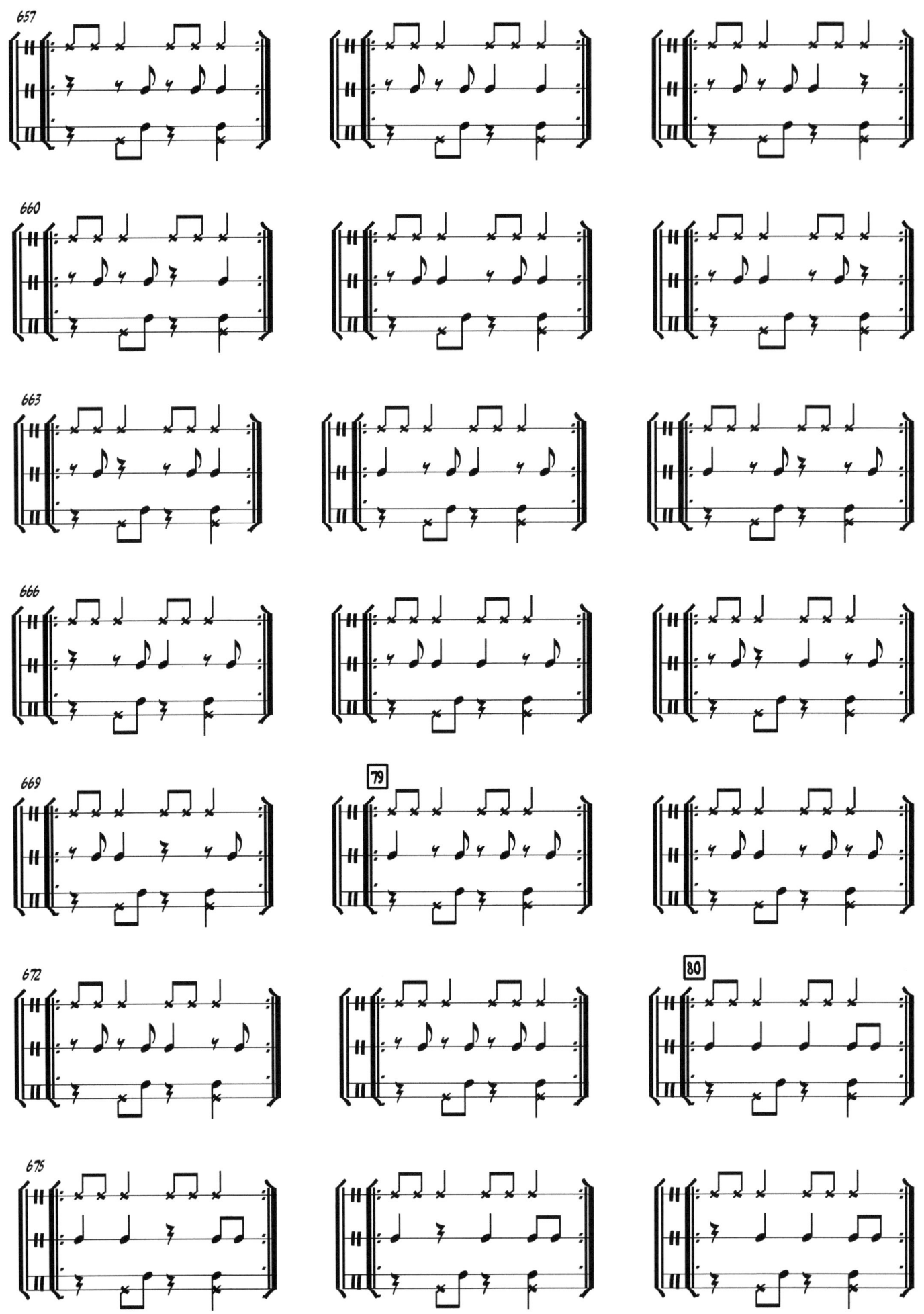

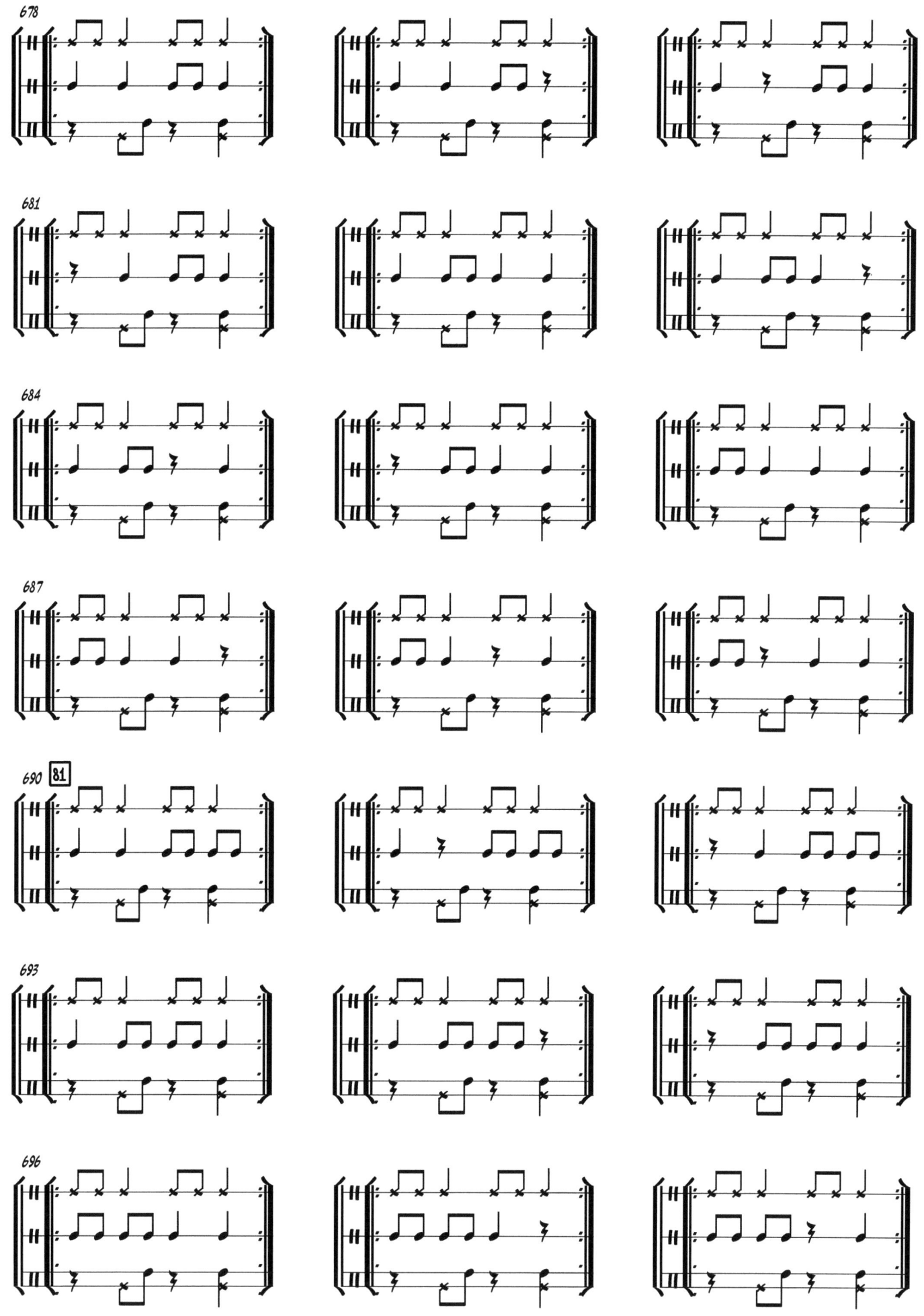

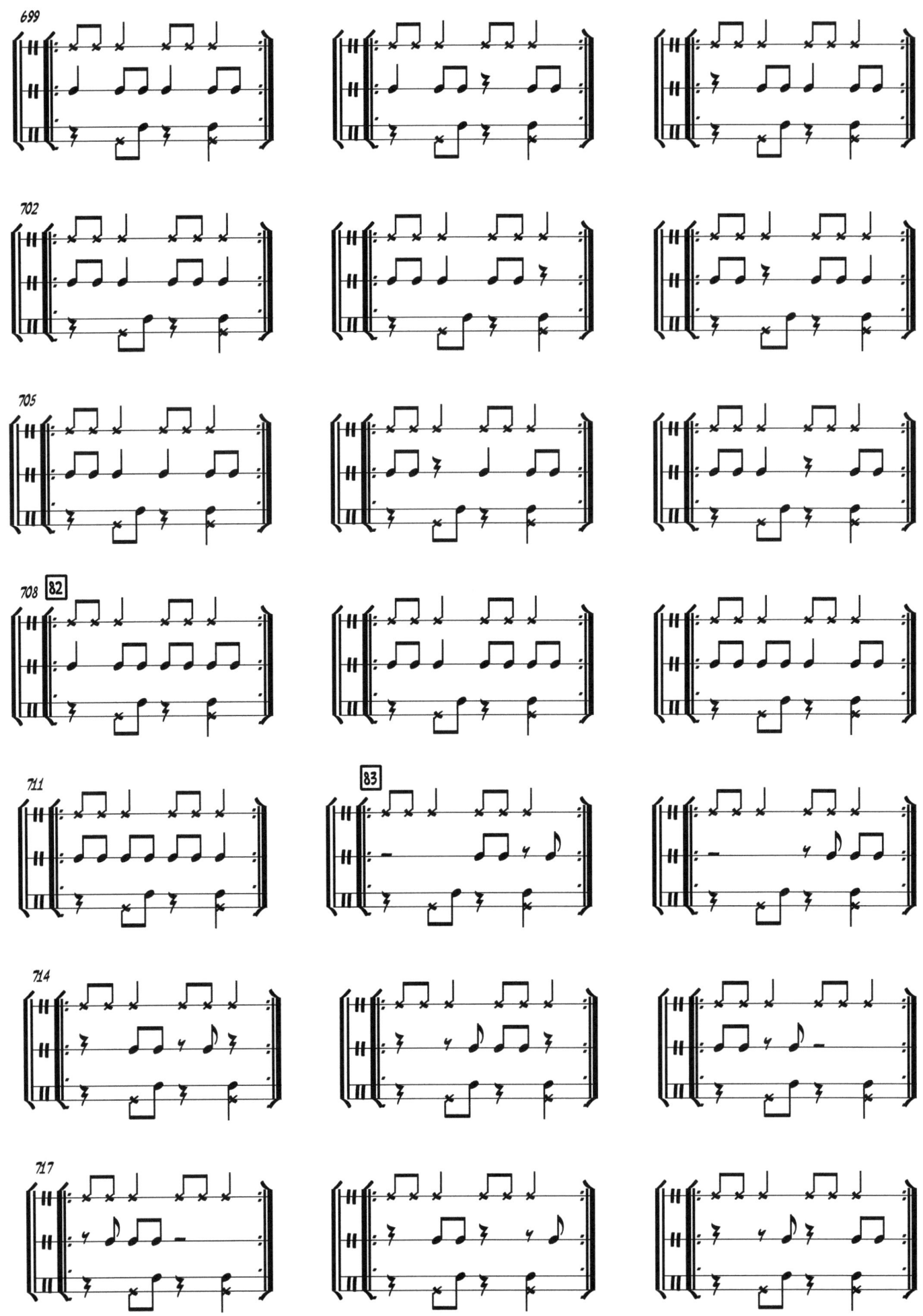

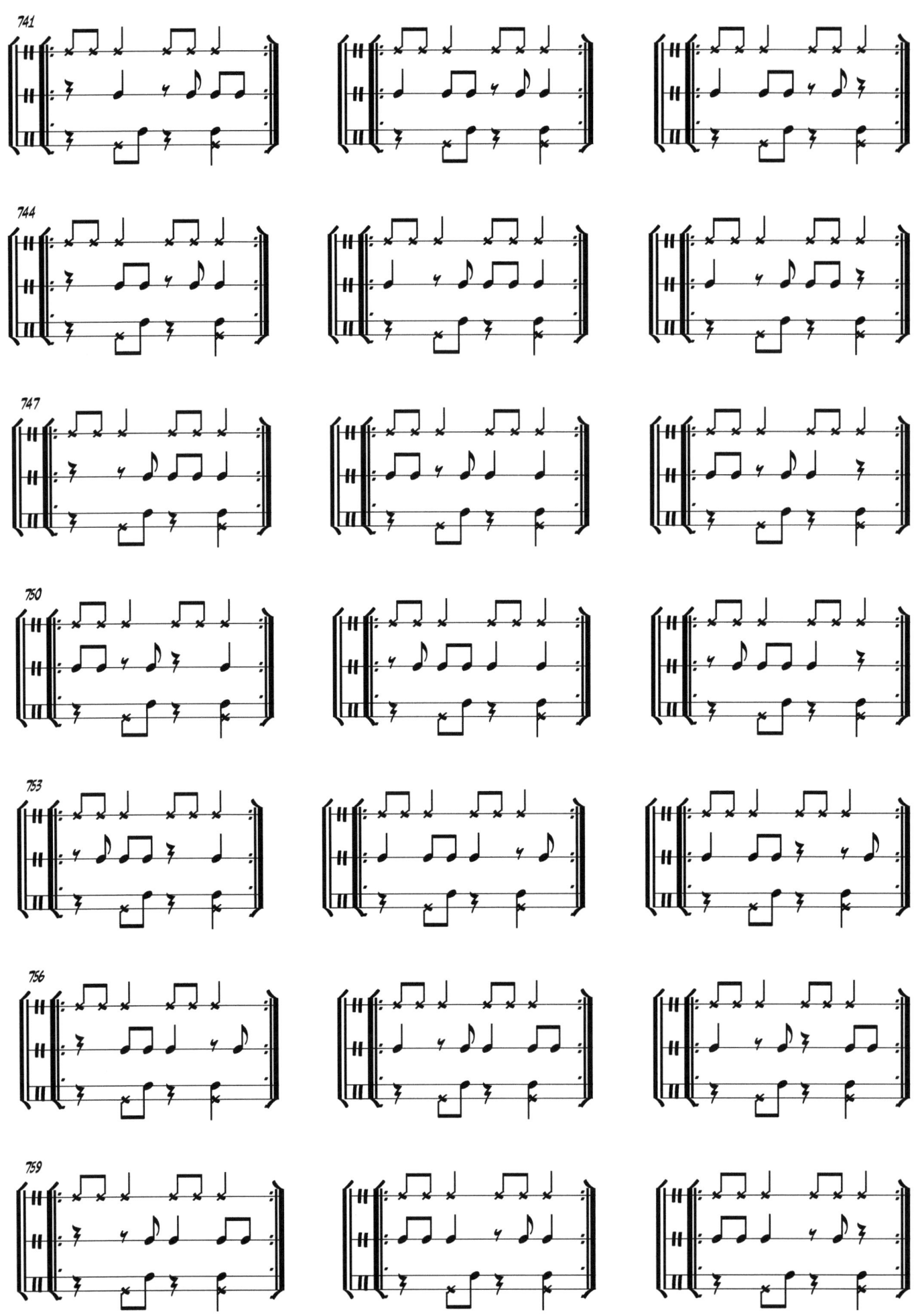

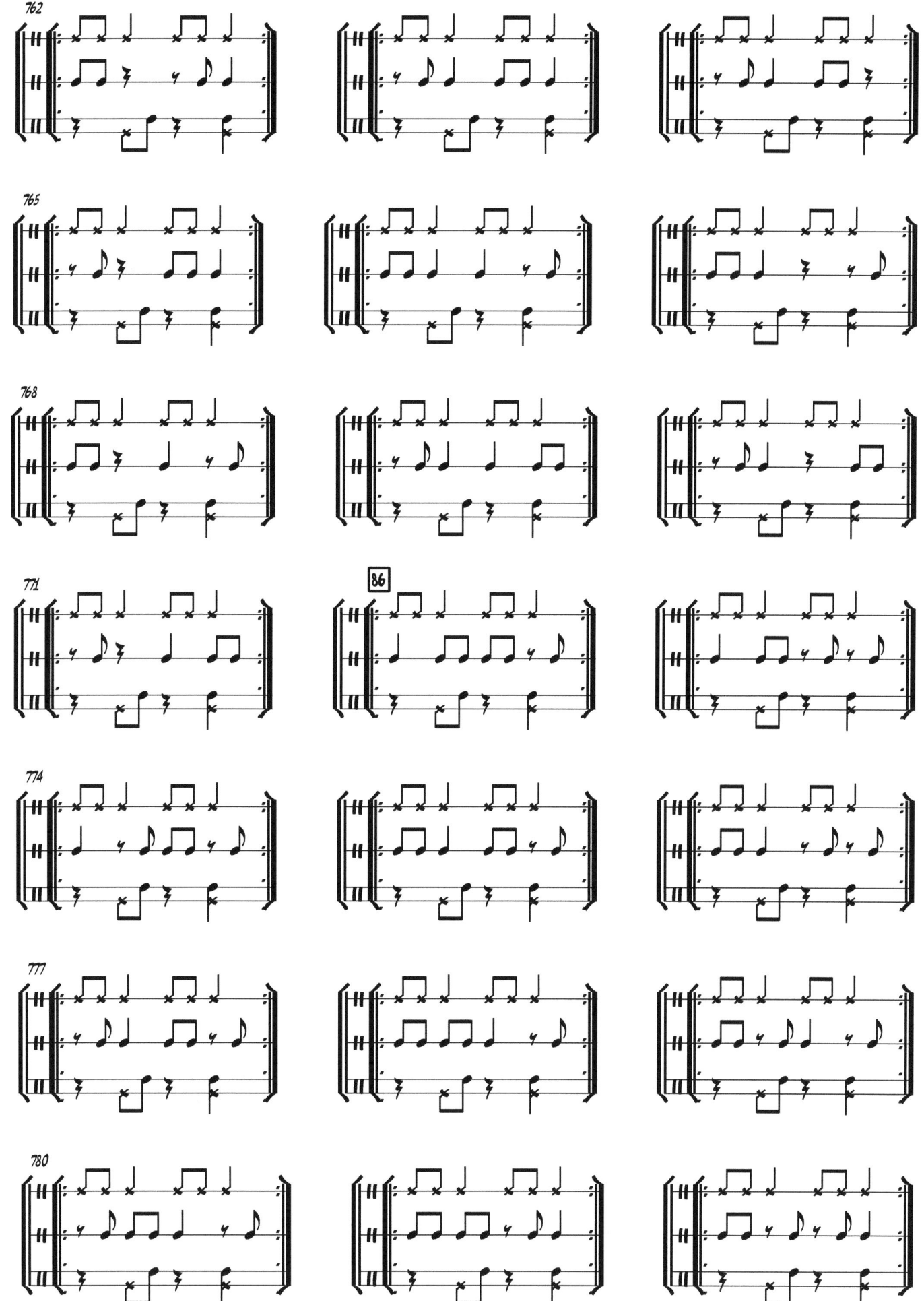

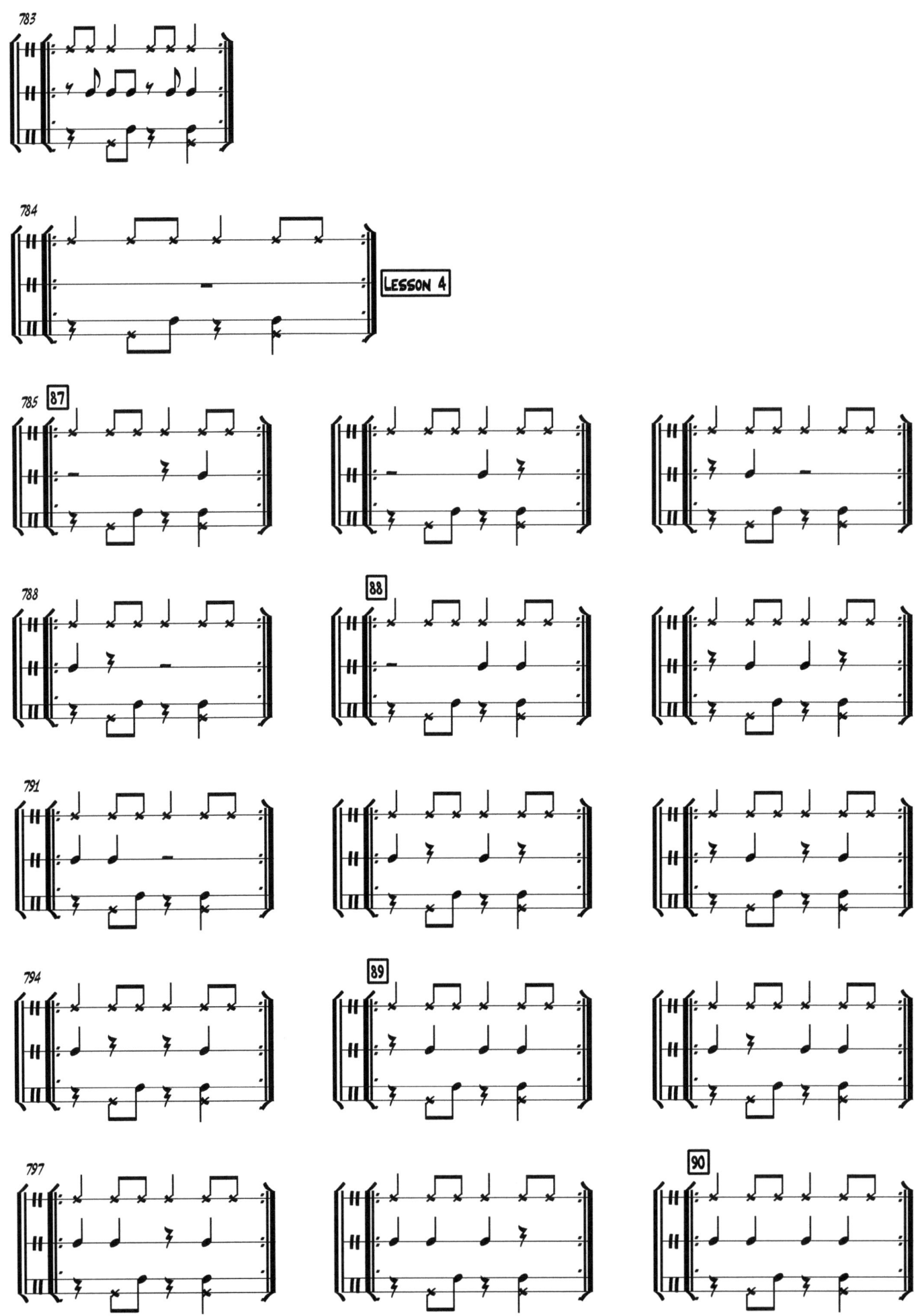

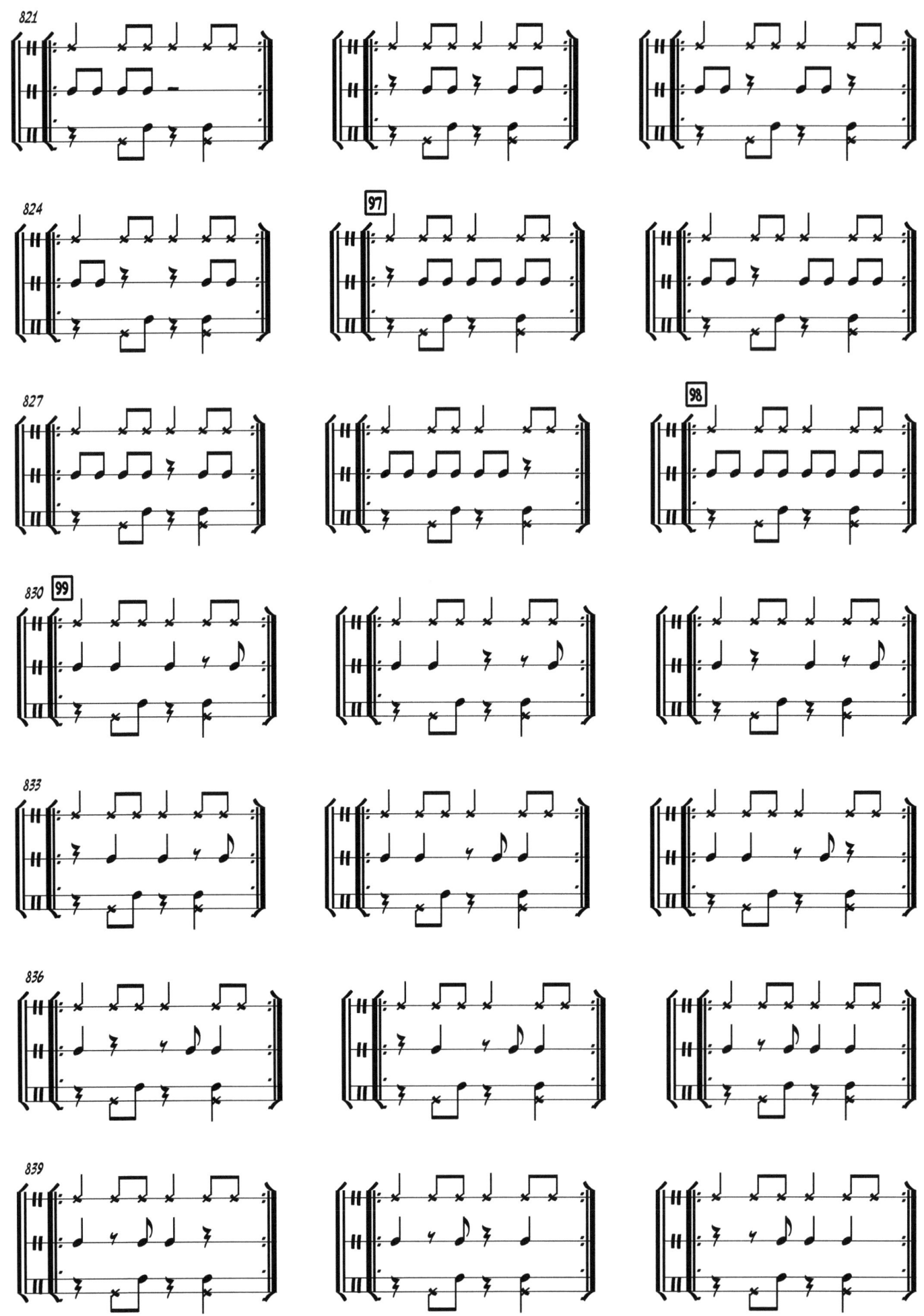

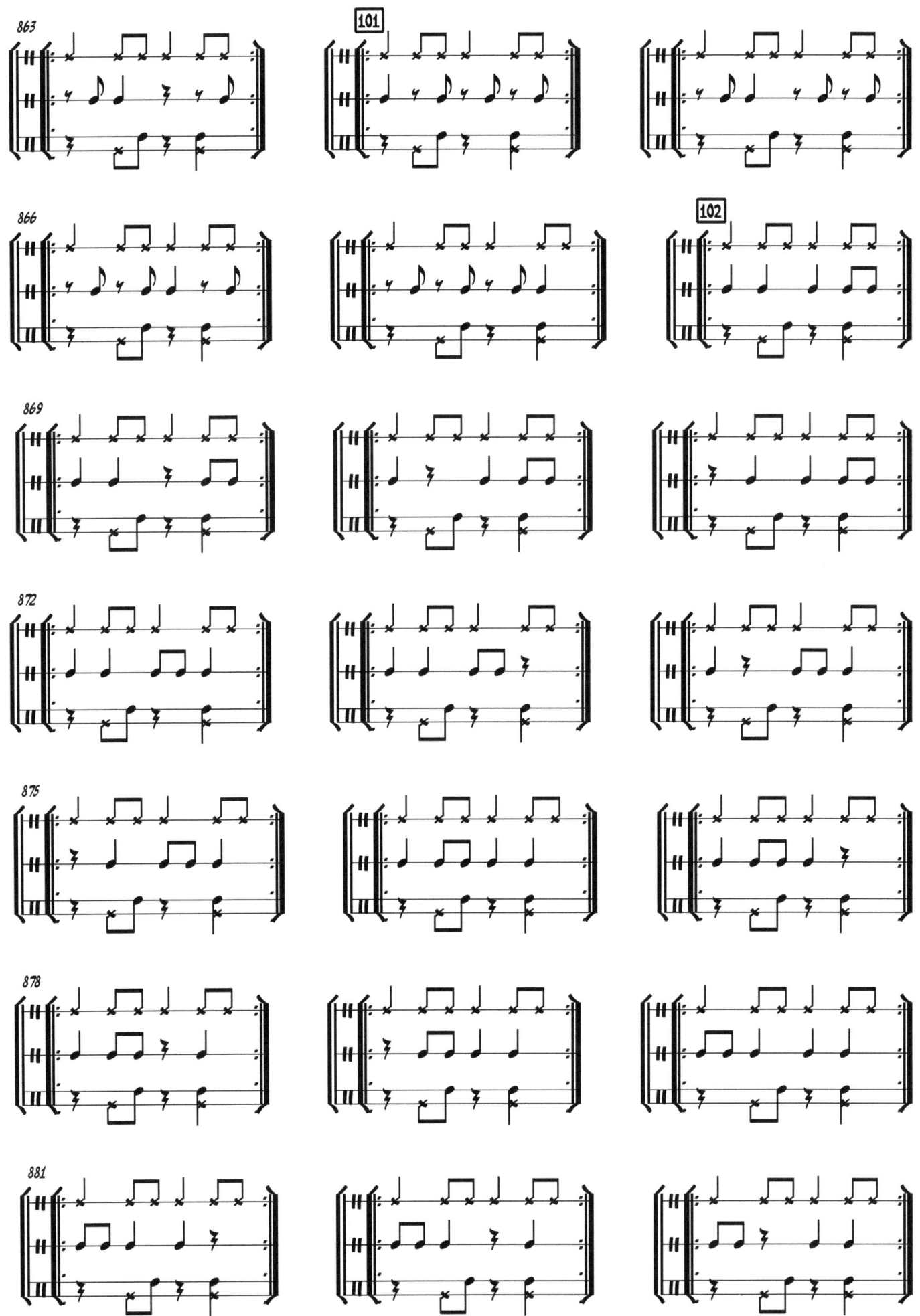

44

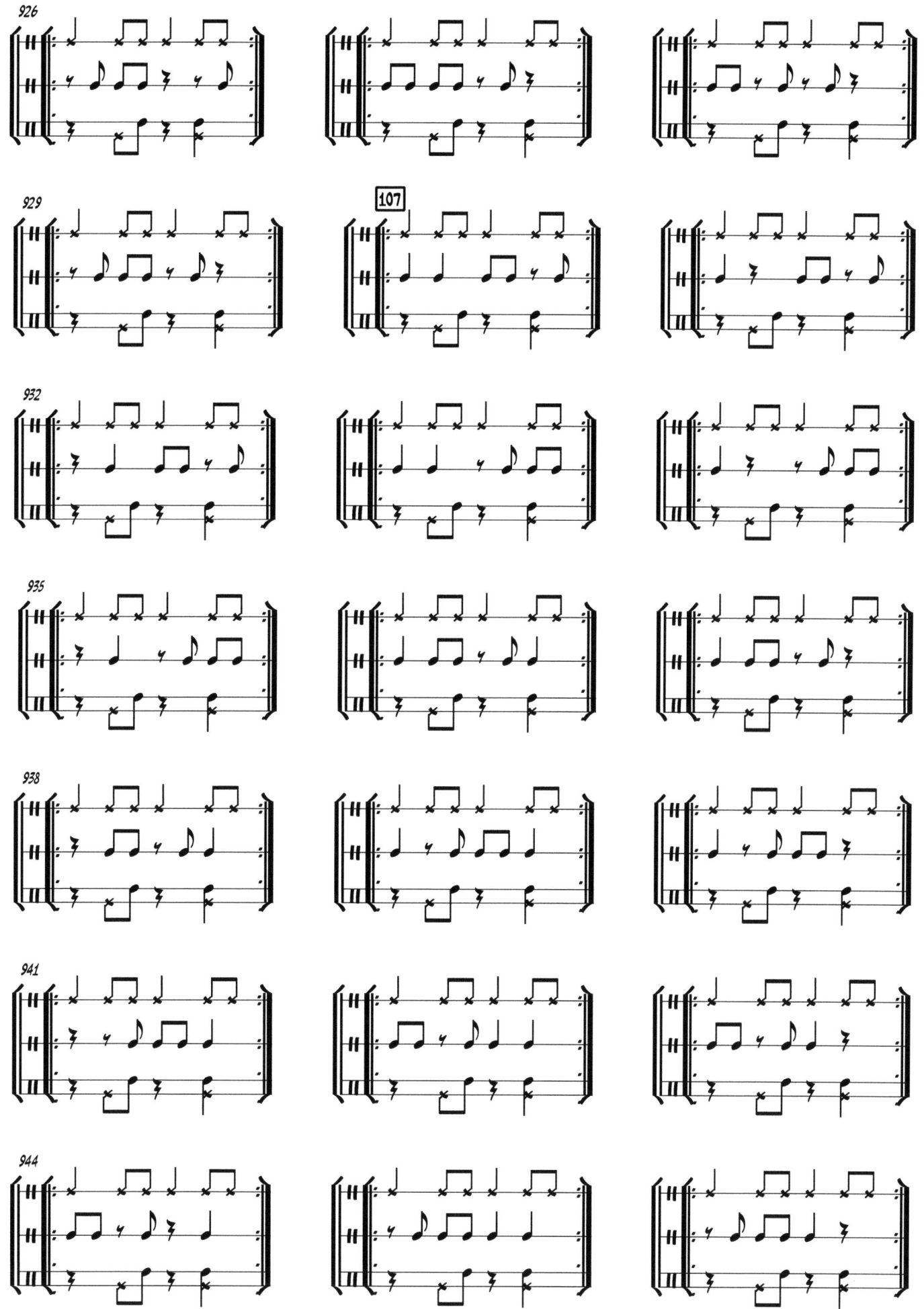

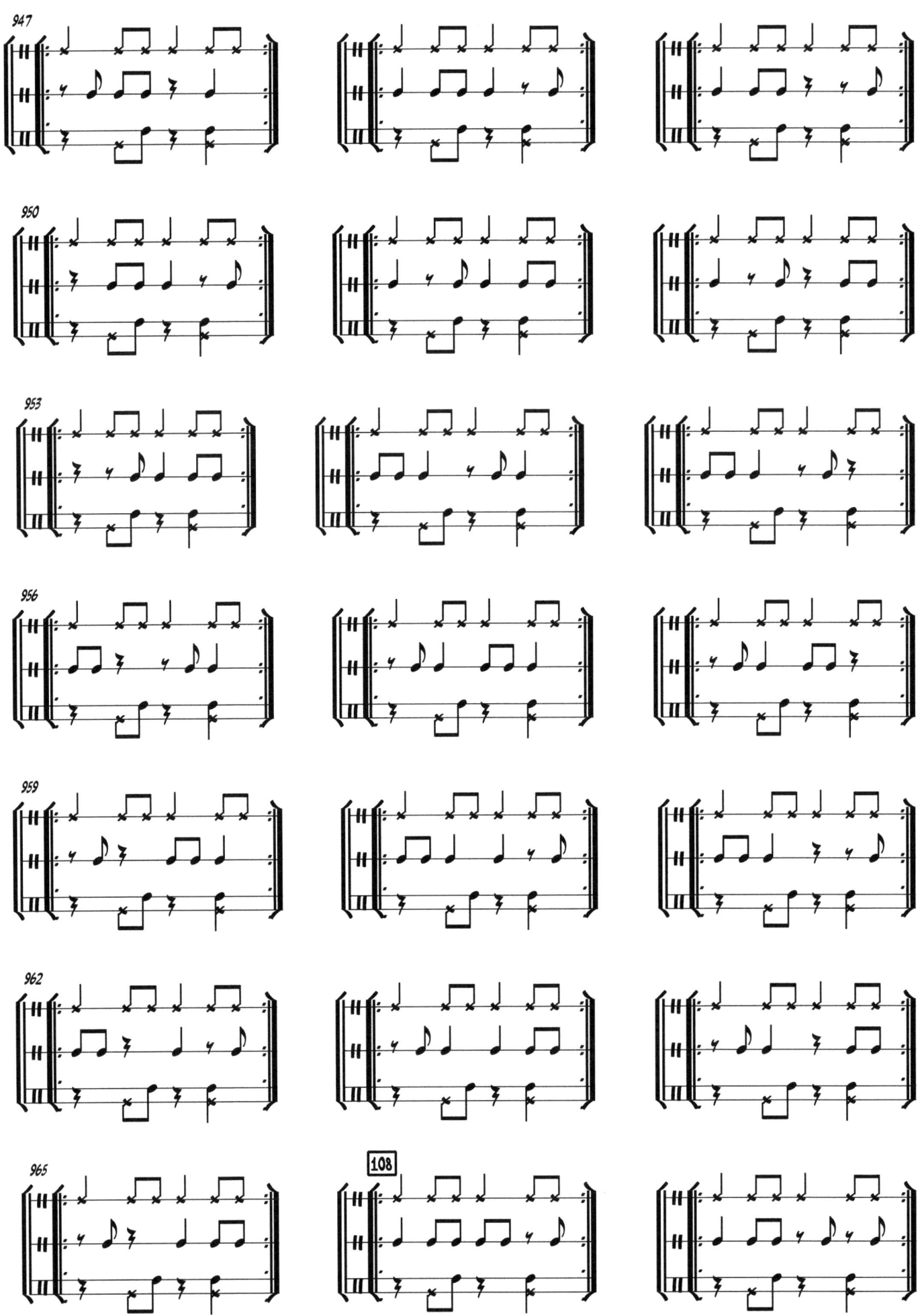

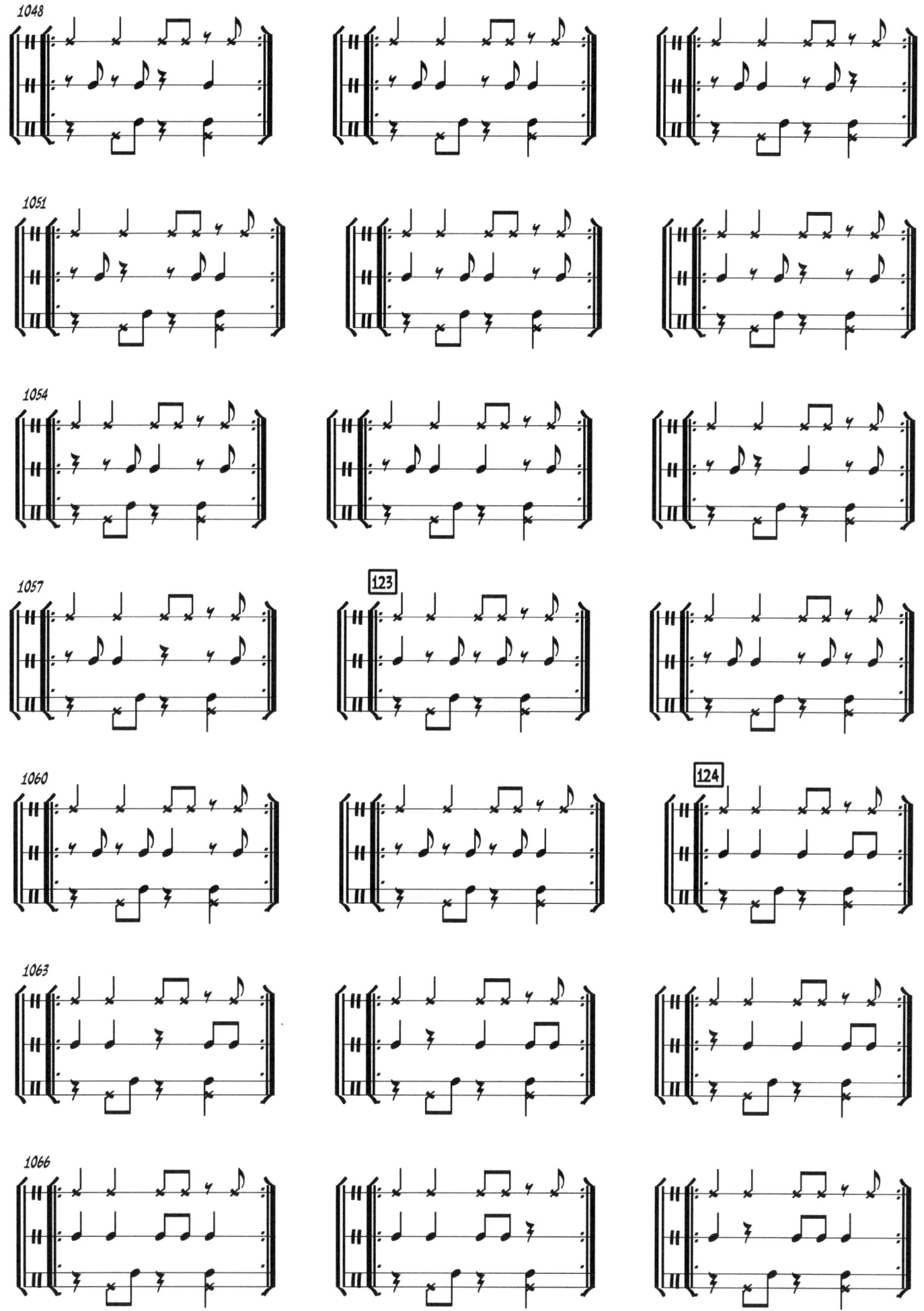

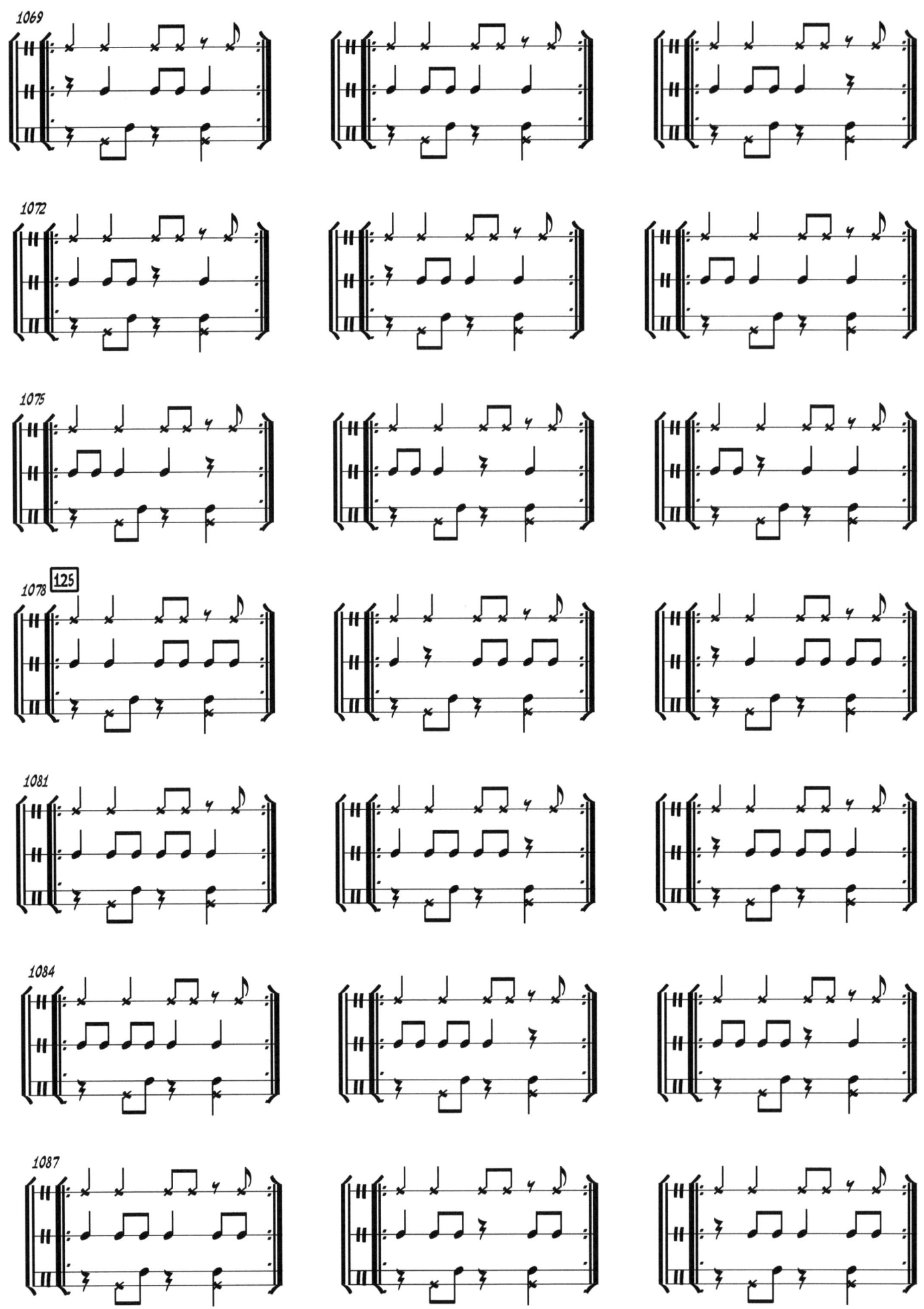

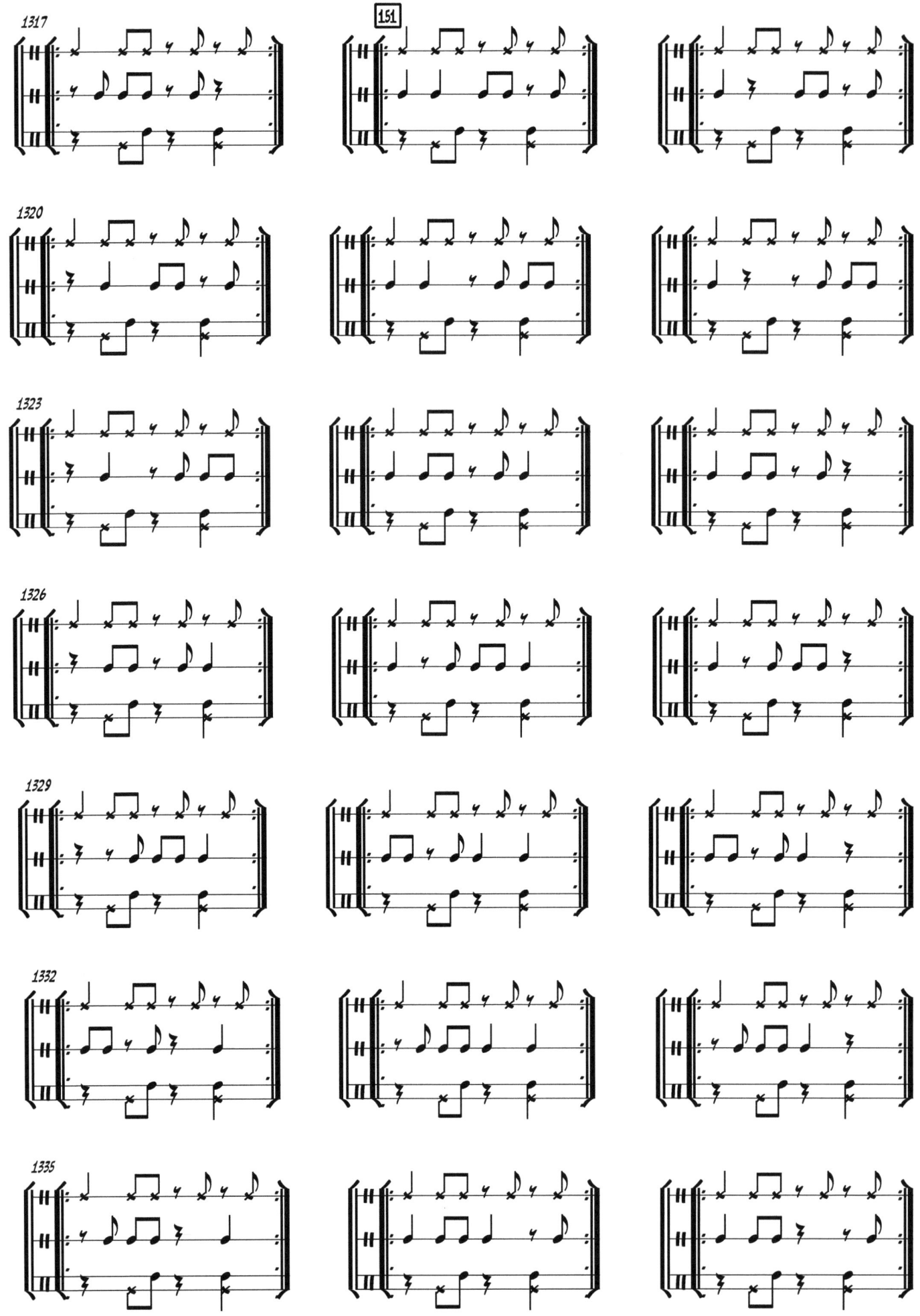

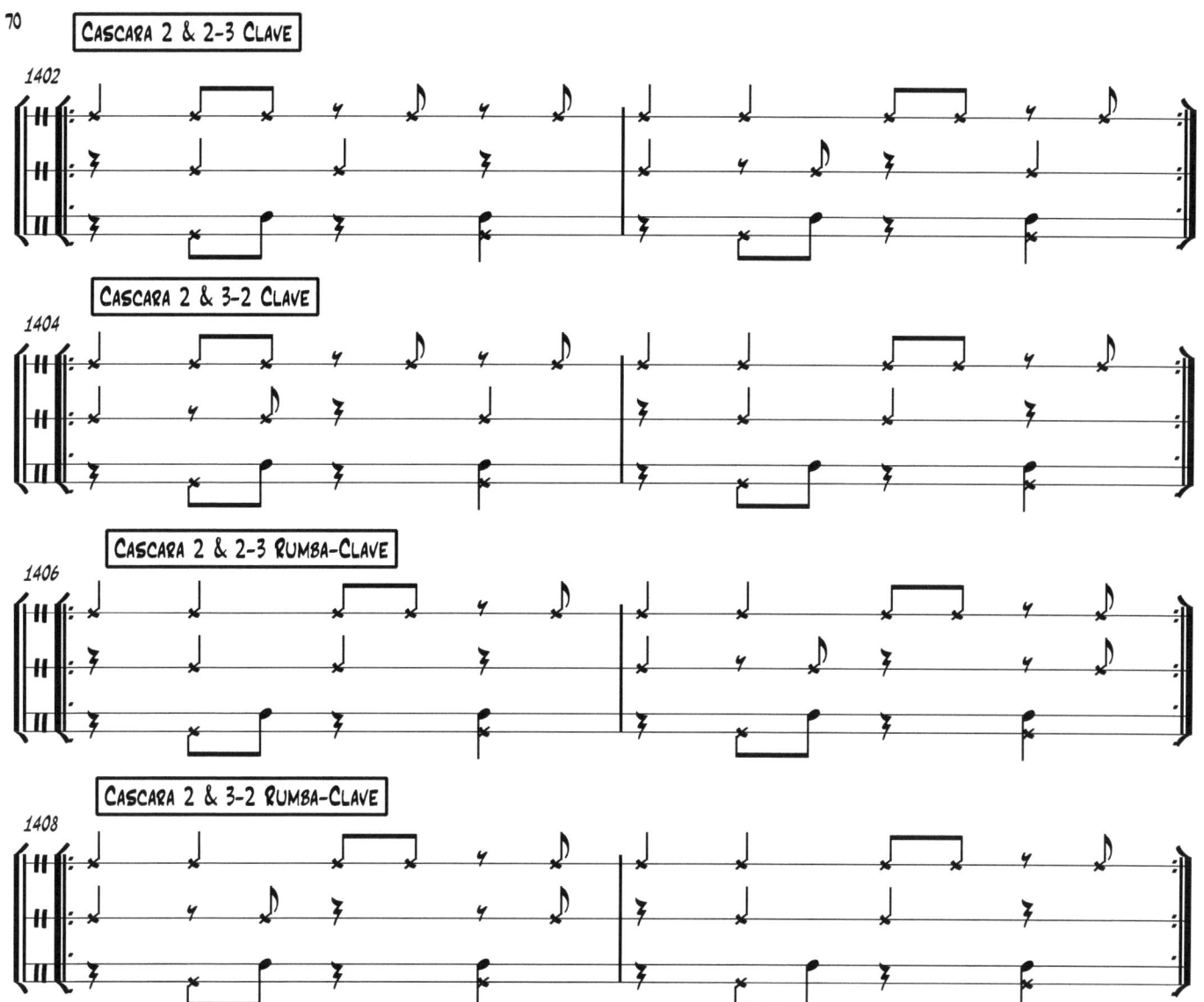